I0605942

DONNA K. MALTESE

Devotions & Prayers *to Rest in God's Presence*

INSPIRATION TO DECLUTTER YOUR MIND & HEART

Print ISBN 979-8-89151-135-4

Text previously appeared in *365 Devotions for a Peaceful Spirit*, published by Barbour Publishing, Inc.

Published by Barbour Publishing, Inc., 1810 Barbour Drive, Uhrichsville, Ohio 44683, www.barbourbooks.com

Our mission is to inspire the world with the life-changing message of the Bible.

Printed in China.

Introduction

Welcome to a breath of fresh air called *Devotions and Prayers to Rest in God's Presence*. Based on timeless wisdom, past and present, this lovely book will be sure to spark your spirit, fire up your imagination, and inspire you to go deeper with your Lord.

Although our world and society are forever changing, God, His Word, and His unsurpassable peace have not. Within these pages, you will find the balm needed to heal your soul as you walk through your days with the Lord of love, Prince of peace, and Spirit of solace. During seasons of hardship, illness, loss, grief, and challenge, you will discover here calm for your clamoring spirit and will rise from each reading with a new perspective, a new promise, a new path, and a new peace.

Within each devotional, you will find a scripture and a thoughtful meditation followed by excerpts of powerful writings, poems, songs, or quotes. May these readings spur you on to living your life with a more peaceful spirit.

Your hearts were stuck in your throats. . . . You didn't know which end was up. Then you called out to God in your desperate condition; he got you out in the nick of time. He quieted the wind down to a whisper, put a muzzle on all the big waves. And you were so glad when the storm died down, and he led you safely back to harbor.

Psalm 107:26–30 msg

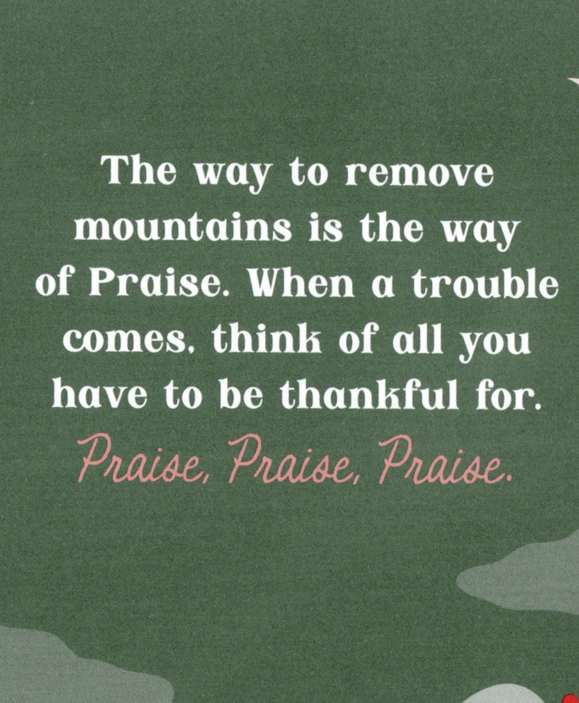
The way to remove mountains is the way of Praise. When a trouble comes, think of all you have to be thankful for.

Praise, Praise, Praise.

Remover of Mountains

He appointed those who should sing to the LORD, and who should praise the beauty of holiness, as they went out before the army.

2 CHRONICLES 20:21 NKJV

King Jehoshaphat and his people had every reason to be afraid. After all, three armies were on their way to annihilate them. They were almost on their doorstep! Fortunately, Jehoshaphat was a humble and godly king. So he knew where to go for help: to God. Before his people, the king prayed, "We have no power against this great multitude that is coming against us; nor do we know what to do, but our eyes are upon You" (2 Chronicles 20:12 NKJV).

God responded by telling Jehoshaphat and his people, "Do not fear or be dismayed; tomorrow go out against them, for the LORD is with you" (2 Chronicles 20:17 NKJV). Following the Lord's guidance, the king instructed the singers to go before his army, praising God. When they came over the rise and could see where the enemy armies had encamped, they saw that they'd destroyed one another. Their faith and praise had removed the mountainous powers against them.

The way to remove mountains is the way of Praise. When a trouble comes, think of all you have to be thankful for. Praise, Praise, Praise.

Say "Thank you" all the time. This is the remover of mountains, your thankful hearts of praise.

God Calling

Safety, Security, and Guidance

He brought me up also out of an horrible pit, out of the miry clay, and set my feet upon a rock, and established my goings.

Psalm 40:2 KJV

Some days you may find yourself in a pit of despair. When you're in that dark place, wait patiently for God to draw you back out into His light. Expect Him to show up to save you. Cry out, knowing He *will* hear your voice and be there before you even utter your first word.

And when God gets there—and He *will* get there—He'll not only save you by pulling you out of the pit, He'll secure you by setting your feet on terra firma. Then He'll guide your next steps, ensuring they'll be steady and solid. Safety, security, and guidance from the Creator of the universe, the one who gives you breath, keeps your world in orbit—what more could you need or want?

You Matter

Meditate upon that wonder—truth, the three steps safety, security, guidance. (1) "He brought me up also out of an horrible pit"—*Safety.* (2) "He set my feet upon a rock"—*Security.* (3) "He established my goings"—*Guidance.* No. 3 is the final stage when the saved soul trusts [God] so entirely it seeks no more its own way but leaves all future plans to [God] its Rescuer.

God Calling

Calming the Storm

Hush now! Be still (muzzled)! And the wind ceased.

Mark 4:39 AMPC

Jesus suggested He and the disciples take the boats to the other side of the lake. On the way, Jesus fell asleep in the stern even after a huge storm rose up and water started filling the boats! So the disciples woke Jesus, saying, "Don't You care if we're about to die?" That's when Jesus got up, calmed the storm, and then asked the disciples, "Where is your faith?"

When worries start to flood into your life, allow faith to anchor you. Remind yourself of Jesus' love and power and of the words of Minister Lloyd John Ogilvie, who said, "Sometimes the Lord rides out the storm with us and other times He calms the restless sea around us. Most of all, He calms the storm inside us in our deepest inner soul."

Worry Less, Pray More

We also often may catch ourselves thinking that Jesus has gone to sleep when storms come on the Church or on ourselves, and that He is ignorant of, or indifferent to, our plight. But though the disciples were wrong in their fright, and not altogether right in the tone of their appeal to Jesus, they were supremely right in that they did appeal to Him. Fear which drives us to Jesus is not all wrong. The cry to Him, even though it is the cry of unnecessary terror, brings Him to His feet for our help.

MacLaren's Expositions

From Thanksgiving to Rest

Thou hast put gladness in my heart. . . . I will both lay me down in peace, and sleep: for thou, LORD, only makest me dwell in safety.

PSALM 4:7–8 KJV

Ending the day with a spirit of thanksgiving turned to God positively impacts you not only spiritually but emotionally, mentally, and physically! That's what today's science says—but the ancient writer of Psalm 4 knew it all along. Yet don't end at thanksgiving! Continue your prayer by asking God to bless those you love. Then put yourself in God's hands as you lie down in peace, knowing He'll watch over you tonight and prepare you for a good day tomorrow.

365 Devotions on the Power of Prayer

We come before Thee, O Lord, in the end of thy day with thanksgiving. Our beloved in the far parts of the earth, those who are now beginning the labours of the day what time we end them, and those with whom the sun now stands at the point of noon, bless, help, console, and prosper them. Our guard is relieved, the service of the day is over, and the hour come to rest. We resign into thy hands our sleeping bodies, our cold hearths, and open doors. Give us to awake with smiles, give us to labour smiling. As the sun returns in the east, so let our patience be renewed with dawn; as the sun lightens the world, so let our lovingkindness make bright this house of our habitation.

ROBERT LOUIS STEVENSON

Peace amid Affliction

He said to him, Go, wash in the Pool of Siloam—which means Sent. So he went and washed, and came back seeing.

JOHN 9:7 AMPC

I assure you, Dear Sir, I sympathize deeply in your afflictions. With all my heart I present you before our Lord. I have prayed, and still pray, that if you are called to participate in the sufferings of Jesus Christ, you may partake also of his patience and submission. You will find the Lord at all times near your heart, when you seek him by a simple and sincere desire to do and suffer his will. He will be your support and consolation in this time of trouble, if you go to him, not with fear and agitation of spirit, but with calm, confiding love.

Jesus said to the blind man, whose eyes he anointed with clay, "Go wash in the waters of Siloam"—waters soft and tranquil. O, that you might experience the abiding peace which Christ gives. O, that you might become reduced to the simplicity of the little child! It is the child who approaches the nearest to Jesus Christ. It is the child whom he takes in his arms and carries in his bosom. O, how lovely, how attractive, is child-like simplicity! May the sufferings you are now experiencing, render you, child-like and submissive to all the will of your Father. My ill health forbids my writing more fully. God loves you, and you are very dear to me in him. Amen. Jesus, help.

MADAM GUYON

Time-Worthy Peace

For God is not a God of disorder but of peace.
1 Corinthians 14:33 NLT

You've got a commitment on Saturday, a birthday party for a little one. You've got the gift, the gift bag, and the card but can't find the invitation. You're too embarrassed to call the hostess and ask what time you're supposed to show up. So you spend three days tearing your house apart. You finally call another friend who's going, hoping she hasn't lost *her* invitation. She hasn't. She gives you the show-up time and you do just that. The following Monday, you find your invitation under a pile of papers on your desk. Argh!

Has this, or something similar, ever happened to you? If so, it's time to straighten up your purse, desk, office, house. Doing so will keep you from suffering from disorderly stress and open up your days with some orderly peace.

Stress Less, Pray More

To get yourself out of your current chaos and into God's eternal calm, you need to keep your mind "stayed on" Him. That means to fix your thoughts on Him. To train yourself to meditate on His presence and power. That involves opening up, feasting upon, and meditating on God's Word (Psalm 119:15). Memorizing the verses that really speak to your heart and mind. (Consider beginning with the soothing words of Isaiah 26:3.) Then trust God, committing yourself to Him, leaning on Him, and hoping confidently in Him (Isaiah 26:4).

Transformed

Seeking Things Above

If ye then be risen with Christ, seek those things which are above, where Christ sitteth on the right hand of God. Set your affection on things above, not on things on the earth. For ye are dead, and your life is hid with Christ in God.

COLOSSIANS 3:1–3 KJV

This is a noisy world. It's easy to get caught up in the din of media and the voices and gossip of others. It's even hard to find a decent role model, whether on TV, in the movies, or in "real life." Fortunately, the author of Colossians, the apostle Paul, gives you some good advice in this area. He urges you to seek things above, not here below. To set your heart, desires, and eyes on the things of heaven. To shut out all the worldly distractions by thinking, talking, and focusing on the higher things. Because, after all, you've been called to a higher life in Christ. When you change your thoughts and mind-set to Him, you lift the world.

365 Devotions on the Power of Prayer

We pray shut us out from the world's clamour and the wagging tongues and the noisy booming voices, and the example that would lead us not toward Thee, but toward the world. Save us from it and shut us in with Thee, and may we think and talk and meditate on holy things today. This message now with Thy blessing may grace and mercy and peace be with us through Jesus Christ our Lord.

A. W. TOZER

Rest

Return unto thy rest, O my soul.

Psalm 116:7 KJV

Do you recollect the delicious sense of rest with which you have sometimes gone to bed at night, after a day of great exertion and weariness? How delightful was the sensation of relaxing every muscle and letting your body go in a perfect abandonment of ease and comfort! . . . You no longer had to hold up an aching head or a weary back. You trusted yourself to the bed in an absolute confidence, and it held you up, without effort, or strain, or even thought, on your part. You rested!

But suppose you had doubted the strength or the stability of your bed and had dreaded each moment to find it giving way beneath you and landing you on the floor; could you have rested then? Would not every muscle have been strained in a fruitless effort to hold yourself up, and would not the weariness have been greater than if you had not gone to bed at all?

Let this analogy teach you what it means to rest in the Lord. Let your souls lie down upon the couch of His sweet will, as your bodies lie down in their beds at night. Relax every strain, and lay off every burden. Let yourself go in a perfect abandonment of ease and comfort, sure that, since He holds you up, you are perfectly safe. Your part is simply to rest. His part is to sustain you; and He cannot fail.

HANNAH WHITALL SMITH, *The Christian's Secret of a Happy Life*

Steering to Peace

And lead us not into temptation, but deliver us from evil: For thine is the kingdom, and the power, and the glory, for ever. Amen.

MATTHEW 6:13 KJV

Oh, to be free of temptation. To not be enticed to eat that chocolate cake, lie to improve one's standing, buy that unaffordable item, smoke that cigarette, or get involved in ungodly media. Temptation itself isn't bad, but giving in to it is. Because when temptation is satisfied, God is not. Because when one is drawn away by temptation, the urge can become an automatic habit, leading to a besetting sin that begins to control your life instead of God. So, ask God to cool your desire. Pray for Him to be with you in the storm of temptation. He'll lead you away!

365 Devotions on the Power of Prayer

Blessed are all Thy saints, O God and King, who have travelled over the tempestuous sea of this life and have made the harbour of peace and felicity. Watch over us who are still on our dangerous voyage; and remember such as lie exposed to the rough storms of trouble and temptations. Frail is our vessel, and the ocean is wide; but as in Thy mercy Thou hast set our course, so steer the vessel of our life towards the everlasting shore of peace, and bring us at length to the quiet haven of our heart's desire, where Thou, O God, art blessed and livest and reignest for ever. Amen.

SAINT AUGUSTINE

Rest in the Ark

The Lord then said to Noah, "Go into the ark, you and your whole family, because I have found you righteous in this generation."

Genesis 7:1 niv

Suppose that after the ark was completed God said to Noah, "Now, get eight spikes of iron and drive them into the side of the ark." So Noah procured the spikes and did as he was bidden. The word came to him, "Come, you and all your household, and hang on to these spikes." So Noah and his wife, and the three sons and their wives, each held on to a spike. And the rains descended and the flood came, and as the ark was borne up on the waters their muscles were strained to the uttermost.

Imagine God saying to them, "If you hang on till the deluge is over you will be saved!" Can you even think of such a thing as any one of them going safely through?

But, oh, how different the simple Bible story. "And the Lord said to Noah, come thou and all thy house into the ark." That is a very different thing than holding on! Inside the ark they were safe as long as the ark endured the storm. And every believer in Christ is as safe as God can make him. Look away then from all self-effort and trust Him alone. Rest in the ark and rejoice in God's great salvation.

Harry Ironside

Learning Contentment

I have learned, in whatsoever state I am, therewith to be content.

PHILIPPIANS 4:11 KJV

The story is told of a king who went into his garden one morning and found everything withered and dying. He asked the oak tree that stood near the gate what the trouble was. The old oak replied that he was sick of life and was determined to die, because he was not tall and beautiful like the pine. The pine was all out of heart because it could not bear grapes like the vine. The vine was going to throw its life away because it could not stand erect and have as fine fruit as the peach tree; and so on through the garden.

Coming to a little purple violet, the king found its bright face lifted as cheery as ever. "Well, violet, I'm glad amidst all this discouragement to find one brave little flower. You do not seem to be the least disheartened."

"No. I'm really not an important flower, but I believe that if you wanted an oak or a pine or a peach tree or a lilac, you would have planted one; but since I know you wanted a violet, I am determined to be the best violet that I can be."

They who are God's without reserve are in every situation content, for they will do only what He wills and desire to do for Him whatever He desires them to do and be. They strip themselves of everything and in this nakedness find all things restored one hundred fold.

CHARLES SPURGEON

An Opening

Turn ye unto me, saith the LORD of hosts, and I will turn unto you.

ZECHARIAH 1:3 KJV

When, for some reason—grief, busyness, distractions, troubles—we find ourselves distanced from God as our Companion and Guide, an opening is left in which fear, wrongdoings, selfishness, and weakness can rush in, leaving us feeling bereft of peace. It is then we begin to wonder, *Where is God? Why can I not hear His voice or sense His presence?* The thing is it's not God who has moved. It's us.

God reminds us that we are to "be strong, alert, and courageous" (Haggai 2:4 AMPC). Why? Because He is with us. In fact, His "Spirit stands and abides in the midst" of us (Haggai 2:5 AMPC). Thus we need not fear.

When you sense fear building up, run to God. Turn to Him. Open the door of your heart to Him. As you do so, His presence will return to you, making you strong, calm, and courageous.

Those who have turned to God need ever to turn more into the center of the narrow way. As the soul opens itself more to God, God, whose communication of Himself is ever hindered only by our closing the door of our hearts against Him, enters more into it.

Albert Barnes' Notes on the Whole Bible

Fear not, fear not, all is well. Let the day be full of little prayers to [God], little turnings toward [God]. The smiles of the soul at one it loves.

God Calling

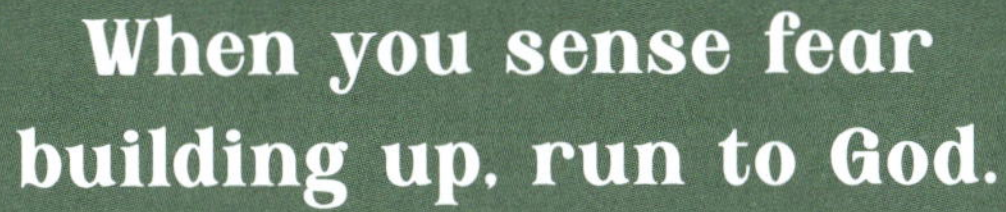

When you sense fear building up, run to God.

Turn to Him.

Open the door of your heart to Him. As you do so, His presence will return to you, making you strong, calm, and courageous.

Continual Fruitfulness

And God Almighty bless thee, and make thee fruitful, and multiply thee, that thou mayest be a multitude of people.

Genesis 28:3 KJV

Years ago you thought you could affect something in your life. You had energy, genius, the grace of oratory, the power of personal attraction, and fascination. You used to be able to sway people; people gathered around you and recognized their born leader. Perhaps you could organize effectively and efficiently. Beneath your word and deft hand all rabble would fall into rank and become a disciplined army. You had the facility of selection—intrepid courage, wise counsel, quick sympathy.

But all this is over now. You are compelled reluctantly to confess that the total residue is disappointing, so you are coming to think that the remainder of your life will never rise above the dead levels of the past, will never achieve any large success for God, will never be fruitful.

"But, I will do my best," you say, "building up believers. If I am unable to perform great feats of winning the ungodly, I can train children, I can share my faith, I can be a channel of love."

To people like this, God comes with His assurance; "I am able to make thee exceeding fruitful."

"Walk before Me, and be thou perfect" (Genesis 17:1).

This is the one prime and irreversible condition for the life which shall become fruitful.

Have we conformed to it?

Then take heart, for it is to such that God says, "I will make thee exceeding fruitful" (Genesis 17:6).

F. B. Meyer

Go Forward Unafraid

Lord, to whom shall we go? Thou hast the words of eternal life.

John 6:68 KJV

Go forward unafraid. Health and Strength, Peace and Happiness and Joy—they are all [God's] gifts. Yours for the asking. In the spiritual (as in the material) world there is no empty space, and as self and fears and worries depart out of your lives, it follows that the things of the Spirit, that you crave so, rush in to take their places.

All things are yours, and ye are Christ's, and Christ is God's. What a wonderful cycle, because ye are God's. Be not afraid. Fear not. It is to the drowning man the Rescuer comes. To the brave swimmer who can fare well alone He comes not. And no rush of Joy can be like that of a man toward his Rescuer. It is a part of [God's] method to wait till the storm is at its full violence. So did [Jesus] with [His] disciples on the lake. [He] could have bidden the first angry wave be calm, the first gust of wind be still, but what a lesson unlearned. What a sense of tender nearness of refuge and safety would have been lost.

Remember this—[Jesus'] disciples thought that in sleep [He] had forgotten them. Remember how mistaken they were. Gain strength and confidence and joyful dependence and anticipation from that. Never fear. Joy is yours, and the radiant Joy of the rescued shall be yours.

God Calling

Shelter from Life's Storms

Then they cry unto the LORD in their trouble, and he bringeth them out of their distresses. He maketh the storm a calm, so that the waves thereof are still. Then are they glad because they be quiet; so he bringeth them unto their desired haven.

PSALM 107:28–30 KJV

When the storms of life rise up, hunker down into your refuge, the rock of God. Cry out, and He'll bring you out. Even better, He'll still the waves, calm the wind. Jesus did it for His disciples when their boat was rocked. He'll do it for you too. So flee to the One who has power over all creation. Allow Him to calm you. When you do, you'll reach just what you've been striving for, that desired haven—peace in God within, no matter what befalls you without. Pray:

Almighty God, the Refuge of all that are distressed, grant unto us that, in all trouble of this our mortal life, we may flee to the knowledge of Thy lovingkindness and tender mercy; that so, sheltering ourselves therein, the storms of life may pass over us, and not shake the peace of God that is within us. Whatsoever this life may bring us, grant that it may never take from us the full faith that Thou art our Father. Grant us Thy light, that we may have life, through Jesus Christ our Lord. Amen.

GEORGE DAWSON, *365 Devotions on the Power of Prayer*

The Peace of a Heavenly Home

"There is plenty of room for you in my Father's home."

John 14:2 msg

We are expecting that one of these days, if the chariot and horses of fire do not stop at our door, our dear Lord and Savior will fulfill His promise to us, "If I go and prepare a place for you, I will come again, and receive you unto myself; that where I am, there ye may be also" (John 14:3 kjv).

To a true believer in Jesus, the thought of departing from this world and going to be "forever with the Lord" has no gloom associated with it. Heaven is our home. We are longing for the great reunion with our beloved Lord, from whom we shall then never be separated.

I cannot attempt to depict the scene when He introduces us to the principalities and powers in heavenly places and invites us to sit with Him. Surely then, the holy angels, who have never sinned, will unite in exclaiming, "Behold, how He loved them!" It is a most blessed thought, to my mind, that we may be up there before the hands of that clock complete another round. If not that soon, it will not be long before all of us who love the Lord will be with Him where He is. Then the last among us shall know more of His love than the greatest of us can ever know while here below.

Charles Spurgeon

Careful for Nothing

Be careful for nothing; but in every thing by prayer and supplication with thanksgiving let your requests be made known unto God. And the peace of God, which passeth all understanding, shall keep your hearts and minds through Christ Jesus.

PHILIPPIANS 4:6–7 KJV

Our vision is limited. We cannot see the future and are at times uncertain of the present. If we are not focused on or looking for God's working, our imaginations can run away with us. Soon we are thinking of the worst-case scenario, reasoning that we should, after all, be prepared just in case. Before we know it, our thoughts careen out of control. Next our emotions respond, and we sink in despair over an imagined outcome that may never be realized!

We are to live "careful for nothing" (Philippians 4:6 KJV). Let go of the past, present, and future. God has promised to take care of you. It's not a theory, but fact! Look to the lilies and the birds. If God is taking care of them, He is more than attentive to what those created in His image need, want, desire, and deal with, every moment of every day.

Like a nursing mother, when God hears your every sigh, whine, and cry, He responds immediately. You are His precious baby girl. Trust Him as you trust the earth to support you. You are in His hands, hearts, and thoughts. It is in Christ Jesus—who does all things well—that you will find your peace and rest.

Woman's Secret of a Happy Life

No Worries

"Do not worry about your life. . . . Look at the birds of the air; they do not sow or reap or store away in barns, and yet your heavenly Father feeds them. Are you not much more valuable than they?"

Matthew 6:25–26 NIV

Does not God provide for all the birds and beasts and fishes? Do not the sparrows fly from their bush and every morning find meat where they laid it not? Do not the young ravens call to God, and He feeds them? And were it reasonable that the sons of the family should fear the father would give meat to the chickens and the servants, his sheep and his dogs, but none to them? He would be a very ill father that should do so; or he would be a very foolish son who would think his father would do so.

Besides the reasonableness of this faith and this hope, we have infinite experience of it. How innocent, how careless, how secure, is infancy. And yet how certainly provided for. We have lived at God's charges all the days of our life, and hitherto He has not failed us. We have no reason to be wary about the future. God has given us His Holy Spirit; He has promised heaven to us; He has given us His Son; and we are taught from the scriptures.

Our lesson is this: How should not He with Him give us all things else?

Jeremy Taylor

Remain at Rest

"Now the Lord my God has given me rest on every side."
1 Kings 5:4 niv

Pay attention to what the "circle of eternity" is. The soul has three ways to God. One of them is to seek God in all creatures through multiple "pursuits" and through burning love. This is what King David of the Old Testament meant when he said, "In all things I have found rest." That is, Jesus and you, embraced once by the eternal light—that is *one thing* in the embrace of the eternal light.

The second way is a wayless way that is free and yet bound. On it we are raised up and carried without will and without form above ourselves and all things. . . . This is what Christ meant when He said: "You are a happy man, Peter! Flesh and blood do not enlighten you" (Matthew 16:17).

The third way is indeed called a "way," yet it means being "at home": seeing God directly in His own being. Our dear Christ says, "I am the Way, the Truth, the Life" (John 14:6).

Listen then to this wonder! How wonderful it is to be both outside and inside, to seize and to be seized, to see and at the same time to be what is seen, to hold and to be held—that is the goal where the spirit remains at rest, united with eternity.

Meister Eckhart

"Peace, Peace"

You will keep him in perfect peace, whose mind is stayed on You.

Isaiah 26:3 NKJV

If you sometimes fall, do not lose heart or cease striving to make progress, for even out of your fall, God will bring good; just as a man selling an antidote will drink poison before he takes it in order to prove its power.

If nothing else could show us what wretched creatures we are and what harm we do to ourselves by dissipating our desires, this war that goes on within us would be sufficient to do so and lead us back to recollection. . . . What hope can we have of being able to rest in others, if we cannot rest in ourselves?

None of our friends and relatives are as near to us as our own personal selves. Whether we like it or not, there are times when even our personal faculties seem to be making war upon us, as if they were resentful of the war made upon them by our personal vices.

"Peace, peace," said the Lord; words He spoke many times to His apostles. Unless we are at peace and strive for peace within ourselves, we shall not find it in others. Let this war cease. By the blood that Christ shed for us, I beg this of those who have not begun to enter within themselves. Those who have begun to do so must not allow such warfare to turn them back. Let them place their trust, not in themselves, but in the mercy of God.

TERESA OF AVILA

Good News

The Lord gives the word [of power]; the women who bear and publish [the news] are a great host. . . . How beautiful upon the mountains are the feet of him who brings good tidings, who publishes peace, who brings good tidings.

Psalm 68:11; Isaiah 52:7 AMPC

When you are weary, when you can no longer keep your eyes open, when you cannot find the energy to lift your head, when you are bluer than blue and sadder than sad, when you're all these things and have yet to get out of bed, it's time to reconsider what you're considering.

You are a wonderful and beautiful creation of God. You are one of His great masterpieces. And your wonder and beauty lie in remembering you are also a daughter of a King. Tap into God. Ask Him to give you the power to rise, the joy to fly, and the energy to walk with a lilt in your step as you publish peace and spread His message of love through your smile, calmness, confidence, contentment, and gentle joy.

When you are weary think that yours are the feet of those who bring glad tidings. This will rob your steps of weariness, will give a Joy and a spring to your walk. "Bringeth glad tidings. Publisheth Peace." What a joyful mission. One of gladness and Peace. Never forget this, and the Joy of your message and mission will radiate from you, gladdening and transforming.

God Calling

Eyes on Jesus

Keep your eyes on Jesus, who both began and finished this race we're in. Study how he did it. Because he never lost sight of where he was headed—that exhilarating finish in and with God—he could put up with anything along the way.

Hebrews 12:2 msg

Moses brought God's children to the borders of Canaan, went atop Mount Pisgah to view the Promised Land, and then died on that lofty height (Deuteronomy 34). Commenting on this story, Matthew Henry wrote that God's law brings His people "into the wilderness of conviction, but not into the Canaan of rest and settled peace." That "spiritual rest of conscience and the eternal rest in heaven" can only be accessed through Jesus.

Thus, the Promised Land is not an actual *place* but the *person* of Christ, the reward received when women of the Way accept Him as Lord of their life and then abide in Him—here on earth and someday in heaven. To reach that Promised Land, God's daughters dare not allow earthly things and people to distract them, but merely look to Jesus to lead them through the wilderness. Focused on Christ, woman has all the manna and living water needed for the journey. No longer preoccupied with or drawn away by the trappings of this world, she rises to a lofty height to view her true home. There, abiding in the love and light of Christ, she reaches her peace of the Promised Land.

Sweet Hour of Prayer

"Lord, here I am,
claiming and holding on to
Your eternal peace."

Peace from the Inside Out

"Your threat means nothing to us. If you throw us in the fire, the God we serve can rescue us. . . . But even if he doesn't, it wouldn't make a bit of difference, O king. We still wouldn't serve your gods or worship the gold statue you set up."

DANIEL 3:16–18 MSG

Shadrach, Meshach, and Abednego refused to worship King Nebuchadnezzar's idol, so he threatened to throw them into a furnace. But the three men refused to lose their peace about it. They knew and trusted that their God could rescue them. And if He didn't, so be it.

We often want God to change our situation, to beam us up out of our trouble. But He wants to change our mindset. He wants us to stay where we are and remain calm, cool, and collected. For our calm doesn't come from the outside in. It comes from the inside out.

No matter what your circumstances, don't let your fears and anxieties get the best of you. Keep your faith and your peace. You may have to walk through fire, but Christ will be there with you, and you'll come out unharmed (Daniel 3:25–29)!

Today, pray, "Lord, here I am, claiming and holding on to Your eternal peace."

Worry Less, Pray More

Shadrach, Meshach, and Abednego. . .appear to have answered promptly, and without hesitation. . . . They calmly looked at their own duty, and resolved to do it, leaving the consequences with the God whom they worshipped.

Barnes' Notes on the Bible

Fear Not

Fear not, little flock; for it is your Father's good pleasure to give you the kingdom.

LUKE 12:32 KJV

When we begin to be fearful, our peace flies right out the window. To maintain your calm and stave off your fear, tune in to your Shepherd's song.

The music of the shepherd's voice. A comforting word, and how tender. His flock, a little flock, a feeble flock, a fearful flock, but a beloved flock, loved of the Father, enjoying His "good pleasure," and soon to be a glorified flock, safe in the fold, secure within the kingdom. How does He quiet their fears and misgivings? As they stand panting on the bleak mountainside, He points His crook upward to the bright and shining gates of glory and says, "It is your Father's good pleasure to give you these." What gentle words! What a blessed consummation! Gracious Savior, Your gentleness has made me great.

Believers, think of this: "It is your Father's good pleasure." The Good Shepherd, in leading you across the intervening mountains, shows you signals and memorials of paternal grace. Let the melody of the Shepherd's voice fall gently on your ear—"It is your Father's good pleasure." *I have given you,* He seems to say, *the best proof that it is mine. In order for you to have that kingdom, I died for you!*

"As a shepherd seeks out his flock. . . ," says God, "so I will seek out my sheep and will deliver them" [Ezekiel 34:12].

JOHN MACDUFF

On Eagles' Wings

As an eagle. . .carrying them on its wings,
so the Lord alone led him.
Deuteronomy 32:11–12 NKJV

The mother eagle teaches her little ones to fly by making their nest so uncomfortable that they are forced to leave it and commit themselves to the unknown world of air outside. And just so does our God to us. He stirs up our comfortable nests and pushes us over the edge of them, and we are forced to use our wings to save ourselves from fatal falling. Read your trials in this light and see if you cannot begin to get a glimpse of their meaning. Your wings are being developed.

I knew a lady whose life was one long strain of trials. . . . She was driven to use her wings and fly to God. . . . Her wings grew so strong from constant flying that. . .when the trials were at their hardest, it seemed to her as if her soul was carried over them on a beautiful rainbow and found itself in a peaceful resting place on the other side.

With this end in view we can surely accept with thankfulness every trial that compels us to use our wings, for only so they can grow strong and large and fit for the highest flying. Unused wings gradually wither and shrink and lose their flying power; and if we had nothing in our lives that made flying necessary, we might perhaps at last lose all capacity to fly.

Hannah Whitall Smith, *The Christian's Secret of a Happy Life*

God's Calm Eternity

Do not fret.

PSALM 37:1 NKJV

Worry can eat up your life. In fact, the word *fret*, a synonym for worry, comes from the Old English *fretan*, which means to "devour, feed upon, consume"! The remedy for worry is to go to the God who resides within your heart. Spend time in His calming presence. Reawaken your awareness of how much bigger He is than your troubles. In Him you'll find all the hope and power you need to ward off worry—and more.

365 Devotions on the Power of Prayer

God of our secret life, weary of ourselves, we come to Your shelter. Our span of troubled days we bring within Your calm eternity. Over our path of pilgrimage, we feel the spaces of Your immensity. In the strife of life and the sadness of mortality, we find a spirit of power and of hope in Your providence. Infinite Ruler of creation, whose spirit dwells in every world: we look not to the heavens for You, though You are there; we search not in the oceans for Your presence, though it murmurs with Your voice; we wait not for the wings of the wind to bring You near, though they are Your messengers; for You are in our hearts, O God. You make Your abode in the deep places of our thought and love. In each gentle affection, each contrite sorrow, each noble aspiration, we would worship You.

JAMES MARTINEAU

True Trust

Peace I leave with you; My [own] peace I now give and bequeath to you. . . . Do not let your hearts be troubled, neither let them be afraid. [Stop allowing yourselves to be agitated and disturbed; and do not permit yourselves to be fearful and intimidated and cowardly and unsettled.]

John 14:27 AMPC

You have some control over your own peace of heart, mind, body, and soul. Yet to obtain that peace, you *must* leave all things in His capable hands and truly trust Him with the outcome of all.

I remember once standing by the side of a little Highland loch on a calm autumn day, when all the winds were still, and every birch-tree stood unmoved, and every twig was reflected on the steadfast mirror, into the depths of which Heaven's own blue seemed to have found its way. That is what our hearts may be, if we let Christ put His guarding hand round them to keep the storms off, and have Him within us for our rest. But the man who does not trust Jesus is like the troubled sea which cannot rest [Isaiah 57:20], but goes moaning round half the world, homeless and hungry, rolling and heaving, monotonous and yet changeful, salt and barren—the true emblem of every soul that has not listened to the merciful call, "Come unto me, all ye that labour and are heavy laden, and I will give you rest" [Matthew 11:28 KJV].

MacLaren's Expositions

Be Still

Let be and be still, and know
(recognize and understand) that I am God.

Psalm 46:10 AMPC

When you're exhausted, chances are it's because you're trying to do things in your own power. Or it may be that you're tired from trying to overcome obstacles that are blocking your way.

God would have you take another path, walk another way. To begin with, you need to let all things be and be still. To rest your hands, mind, legs, thoughts. To stop trying to do things in your own power. To know that God is God. To open the door to Him who has so much more strength than you could ever summon up. To lift your eyes up to the hills, the heavens, for in God is where your help and strength lie (Psalm 105:4; 121:1–3).

Understand that Jesus, the Son of God within you, has the power to still the wind and the waves, to calm the storms that have risen up. Believe that Jesus will do what He has promised, that He is your ultimate power.

But again, begin with letting all else be. And be still. And know. That He is God.

More Jesus

God's Presence with You

My presence shall go with thee, and I will give thee rest.

Exodus 33:14 KJV

God's presence is the safety of a man. If God be with one, who can hurt one? As He said, "If God be for us, who can be against us?" [Romans 8:31]. Now, if so much safety flows from God, how safe are we when God is with us? "The beloved of the LORD," said Moses, "shall dwell in safety by him, and the Lord shall cover him all day long, and he shall dwell between his shoulders" (Deuteronomy 33:12). God's presence keeps the heart awake to joy and will make a man sing in the night (Job 35:10).

What shall I say? God's presence is renewing, transforming, seasoning, sanctifying, commanding, sweetening, and enlightening to the soul! Nothing like it in all the world; His presence supplies all wants, heals all maladies, saves from all dangers; is life in death, heaven in hell, all in all. No marvel, then, if the presence of, and communion with, God, is become the desire of the righteous man. To conclude this, by the presence of God being with us, it is known to ourselves, and to others, what we are. They are then best known to themselves. They know they are His people because God's presence is with them. Therefore he saith, "My presence shall go with thee, and I will give thee rest."

JOHN BUNYAN

Peace in Forgiveness: Part 1

"Be easy on people; you'll find life a lot easier."

Luke 6:37 msg

It has been said that refusing to forgive someone who injures you is like drinking poison and expecting the offender to die. . . . But if we know there is freedom in forgiveness, why does it seem so hard? We must ask ourselves, "If Jesus can be stripped naked, beaten, scourged, have nails driven into His hands and feet, hang on a cross until death, and still say, 'Father, forgive them for they know what not they do' (see Luke 23:34), why can't we?" "Oh well," you say, "it was easy for Him. He was God." Yet God insists we forgive others no matter how big or small the offenses. But how do we tap into His power of forgiveness?

First. . .allow yourself to feel the hurt of the offenses against you, both past and present. Pray for the release of that hurt, then pray for the power to forgive as God constantly and consistently forgives you. Continue to pray until you've truly forgiven in your heart. (It may not happen immediately, but it *will* happen.) Then thank God for His goodness and peace. Finally, when the time is right, try to restore your relationship with the person who hurt you. Pray for the right words to say. . . . All the while, keep in mind that, although your offender's behavior may not change, you will, becoming more like Christ!

Power Prayers to Start Your Day

Peace in Forgiveness: Part 2

"I have prayed for you, Simon, that your faith may not fail. And when you have turned back, strengthen your brothers."

LUKE 22:32 NIV

Sometimes the one you need to forgive is yourself. Remember how Peter claimed he would never deny Christ and then turned around and did it not once but *three* times? On that third go-around, Peter cried bitterly (Luke 22:62). Perhaps what helped get him past his bitterness was the positive Jesus planted in his mind before the cockcrow. For Jesus had told him that once he'd denied Him, to turn back and strengthen his fellow disciples.

If you have offended yourself or God, talk to Him, pouring out your heart. Ask for His forgiveness, and then try to do better the next time. Don't constantly berate yourself for your bad behavior, toward either yourself or others. God does not forgive us based on how well we perform or how acceptable we believe we are in His sight. He forgives us based on the sacrifice of Jesus Christ. Oswald Chambers wrote, "Forgiveness means not merely that I am saved from sin and made right for heaven. . . . Forgiveness means that I am forgiven into a recreated relationship, into identification with God in Christ."

Don't poison yourself with the bitter pill of *unforgiveness*—it's suicide! Instead, tap into the power of *forgiveness*, keeping Jesus' peace in mind, His mercy in your heart, His power at hand, and your relationships whole.

Power Prayers to Start Your Day

Live in Peace

Jesus said to His disciples, If anyone desires to be My disciple, let him deny himself [disregard, lose sight of, and forget himself and his own interests] and take up his cross and follow Me [cleave steadfastly to Me, conform wholly to My example in living and, if need be, in dying, also].

MATTHEW 16:24 AMPC

Go where we will, if we remain in ourselves, we shall carry everywhere our sins and our distresses. If we would live in peace, we must lose sight of self, and rest in the infinite and unchangeable God. These self-returns have a tendency to establish the soul more and more in itself, and hinder it from running into its great original. But it is to this, God is calling you. You withhold from God the only thing he desires—*the possession of your heart.* The time is short; wherefore spend it in the compass and surroundings of self? The single eye sees only God. You act as a person who being called before a king, instead of regarding the king and his benefits, is occupied only with his own dress and appearance. God wishes to disarrange you—to destroy self; and you wish to preserve what he would destroy. Be more afraid of self than of the evil one. It is the spirit of Satan to exalt self above God, and this spirit is fostered by these continual returns you make upon your own doings and misdoings, which leaves no place in your mind for the occupation of God.

MADAM GUYON

Peace Restored

Isaac prayed hard to GOD for his wife because she was barren. GOD answered his prayer and Rebekah became pregnant. But the children tumbled and kicked inside her so much that she said, "If this is the way it's going to be, why go on living?" She went to GOD to find out what was going on. GOD told her.

GENESIS 25:21–23 MSG

Isaac was forty years old when he took Rebekah to be his wife. Unfortunately, Rebekah turned out to be barren. So Isaac prayed and prayed and prayed about the situation. And then finally God answered his prayer. Rebekah was pregnant! They were overjoyed.

Yet the young woman soon became disturbed. It seemed as if she had warring factions inside her womb. She could have consulted other women. Or Isaac could have once again gone to God. But this time, Rebekah, bereft of peace, went to God for answers. And He soon filled her in on what was going on. Rebekah, the first woman the Bible names as seeking God, knew where to go for wisdom and to seek peace.

Perhaps you too have a problem. Something is disturbing you, confounding your calm. Do as Rebekah did. Before all others, go to God for guidance, knowing "the LORD will guide you continually" (Isaiah 58:11 NKJV). Ask Him to help you understand what's happening. And soon your peace will be restored.

Careful for Nothing

Be careful for nothing; but in every thing by prayer and supplication with thanksgiving let your requests be made known unto God. And the peace of God, which passeth all understanding, shall keep your hearts and minds through Christ Jesus.

PHILIPPIANS 4:6–7 KJV

It cannot be denied that there is no peace without prayer. It's only when we lay everything at our Master's feet can we find clarity, hope, expectation, relief, and the peace that passes anything we can understand or comprehend.

When you find yourself discouraged or troubled, unable to concentrate or find hope, go to the one who commands the water, wind, and waves. Go down on your knees—literally or figuratively. Tell God what's dragging down your spirit, encumbering your heart, and fogging up your mind. Unburden yourself of *everything* that is bothering you. And you will rise up in His peace.

Be careful for nothing.—An exact repetition of our Lord's command, "Take no thought" (in Matthew 6:25; Matthew 6:34). The prohibition is of that painful anxiety which is inevitable in all who feel themselves alone in mere self-dependence amidst the difficulties and dangers of life. It is possible to sink below this anxiety in mere levity and thoughtlessness; it is possible to rise above it by "casting our care on Him who careth for us," and knowing that we are simply "fellow-workers with Him" (1 Peter 5:7; 2 Corinthians 6:1).

Ellicott's Commentary for English Readers

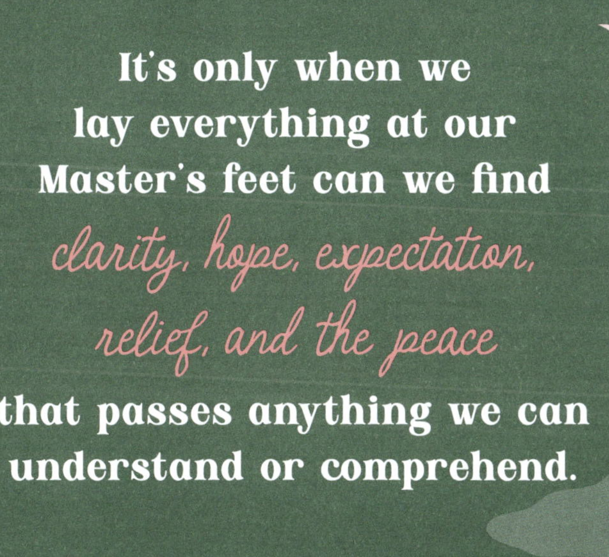
It's only when we
lay everything at our
Master's feet can we find
clarity, hope, expectation,
relief, and the peace
that passes anything we can
understand or comprehend.

A Seeking Heart

You have said, Seek My face [inquire for and require My presence as your vital need]. My heart says to You, Your face (Your presence), Lord, will I seek, inquire for, and require [of necessity and on the authority of Your Word].

Psalm 27:8 AMPC

God wants you to seek His face. For He knows that when you do, your heart, mind, and spirit will have its true focus. You will find His peace, His strength, His way. You will be more in line with His will for you because you have looked to Him before you even set your foot out the door or stuck your toe in the water.

Your spirit needs God's presence as a vital necessity just as your body needs air, food, and water. God's aching to hear your voice. He's ready for that heart-to-heart talk that will energize you for the day. Seek. Speak. Listen. Then walk.

Stress Less, Pray More

We have here a report of a brief dialogue between God and a devout soul. The Psalmist tells us of God's invitation and of his acceptance, and on both he builds the prayer that the face which he had been bidden to seek, and had sought, may not be hid from him. . . .

To hear was to obey: as soon as God's merciful call sounded, the Psalmist's heart responded, like a harp-string thrilled into music by the vibration of another tuned to the same note. Without hesitation, and in entire correspondence with the call, was his response.

MacLaren's Expositions

Looking Good

You'll do best by filling your minds and meditating on things true, noble, reputable, authentic, compelling, gracious—the best, not the worst; the beautiful, not the ugly; things to praise, not things to curse.

PHILIPPIANS 4:8 MSG

One way to have your peace disrupted is to look for trouble where there is none—none worth noting, anyway. Instead of focusing on your faults, or the faults of others, look for the good. Focus on the heart, the love, the joy that is in each person. Look for the light of God behind their eyes. That may require more digging for some than others. But it is there. And it's worth looking for and focusing on.

The true use to be made of all the imperfections of which you are conscious is neither to justify, nor to condemn them, but to present them before God, conforming your will to His, and remaining in peace; for peace is the divine order, in whatever state we may be.

FRANÇOIS FÉNELON

You will find it less easy to uproot faults than to choke them by gaining virtues. Do not think of your faults; still less of others' faults; in every person who comes near you, look for what is good and strong: honor that; rejoice in it; and, as you can, try to imitate it; and your faults will drop off, like dead leaves, when their time comes.

JOHN RUSKIN

Wisdom over Worry

Listen well to my words; tune your ears to my voice.
Keep my message in plain view at all times. Concentrate!
Learn it by heart! Those who discover these words live,
really live; body and soul, they're bursting with health.

Proverbs 4:20–22 msg

David writes that worrying leads to evil and harm (Psalm 37:8). His son Solomon tells you God's wisdom leads to an awesome life. So, if you want the best life, dig into God's wisdom. You'll find it throughout the Bible but especially in Proverbs. There King Solomon provides insight into how to deal with everyday issues, including how to work, act, talk, think, curb your anger, and so much more.

In the verses above, Solomon strongly suggests you learn some verses by heart. Perhaps you could start by reading Proverbs every day. When you come to a verse that really speaks to you, that gives you guidance or peace about a situation, memorize it. Before you know it, God's wisdom will stand in place of your worry.

Worry Less, Pray More

Attentive hearing the word of God, is a good sign of a work of grace begun in the heart, and a good means of carrying it on. There is in the word of God a proper remedy for all diseases of the soul. Keep thy heart with all diligence. We must set a strict guard upon our souls; keep our hearts from doing hurt, and getting hurt. A good reason is given; because out of it are the issues of life.

Matthew Henry's Concise Commentary

God's Peace

The Lord said to him, "Peace be with you. Do not be afraid. You will not die." Then Gideon built an altar there to the Lord. He gave it the name, The Lord is Peace.

JUDGES 6:23–24 NLV

It's a wonder God doesn't throw up His hands at His wishy-washy children.

The Angel of the Lord had come to Gideon, encouraging him to go against all his reason and save Israel from the raiding Midianites, to become who God had created him to be—a mighty warrior.

But the fear-filled Gideon wanted proof that the person he was talking to was really God. Then, when God gave him that proof, Gideon cried out, "I am afraid, O Lord God! For now I have seen the angel of the Lord face to face" (Judges 6:22 NLV). That's when God offered His peace.

Today, fearlessly seek out God, allowing His peace to fall upon your soul.

Gideon realized the momentous character of that interview. He only wanted to be sure that it was no dream or fancy, and so hence the proposal of the flesh and broth. As the fire started forth at the Angel's touch, he knew that the veil of the unseen world had been rent to send him direction and help. At first he was startled, and then the peace of God fell upon his soul. He heard the Voice that uttered a similar benediction in Daniel 10:19 and John 20:26. The peace of God henceforth kept His heart and mind.

F. B. MEYER, *Bible Commentary*

Peace amid the Tempest

The Lord sat enthroned over the flood. . . . The Lord will give power to his people. The Lord will bless his people with peace.

Psalm 29:10–11 GW

Amid the most horrible of storms in our lives, there's a God who will see us through—and beyond.

The God who presides over the tempest and the storm, the God who has such power, and can produce such effects, is abundantly able to uphold His people, and to defend them. In other words, the application of such amazing power will be to protect His people, and to save them from danger. . . . If we feel that God presides over all, and that He controls all this with infinite ease, assuredly we have no occasion to doubt that He can protect us; no reason to fear that His strength cannot support us. . . .

[God] will bless [His people] with peace in the tempest; He will bless them with peace through that power by which He controls the tempest. Let them, therefore, not fear in the storm, however fiercely it may rage; let them not be afraid in any of the troubles and trials of life. In the storm, and in those troubles and trials, he can make the mind calm; beyond those storms and those troubles he can give them eternal peace in a world where no "angry tempest blows."

Barnes' Notes on the Bible

The Peace of Reconciliation

"If you are offering your gift at the altar and there remember that your brother has something against you, leave your gift there before the altar and go. First be reconciled to your brother, and then come and offer your gift."

MATTHEW 5:23–24 ESV

If you're in your place of worship and remember someone has a grudge against you, God wants you to go and make things right. You may have to apologize, forgive, or be forgiven, perhaps even forget the wrong you've done or the wrong done against you. For most of us, this can be an enormous challenge.

Apologizing often takes a lot of courage. Yet God wants you to be the most forgiving and peace-seeking person you can be. So find a way to let the words "I'm sorry" cross your lips. Be sincere when you speak them. Gird yourself with courage, arm yourself with humility and understanding, and make things right.

At the same time, be strong and emboldened enough to forgive all those who have wronged you. And forget the wrong if you can so that you don't sink into a mire of bitterness. For bitterness is like drinking poison and waiting for the other person to die.

Then search yourself and see if there's anything you need to forgive *yourself* for. And do so. Then and only then, make your way back to God. Offer your gift with a pure heart, one now easy, calmed with the peace of reconciliation.

Unafraid

Finding Peace Where We Are

Lot chose for himself all the plain of Jordan, and Lot journeyed east. And they separated from each other. Abram dwelt in the land of Canaan, and Lot dwelt in the cities of the plain and pitched his tent even as far as Sodom.

GENESIS 13:11–12 NKJV

Abram offered Lot his choice. The younger man chose according to the sight of his eyes. In his judgment he gained the world—but see 2 Peter 2:7–8. The world is full of Lots—shallow, impulsive, doomed to be revealed by their choice and end. "Let there be no strife!" Blessed are the peace-makers! Wherever the interests of peace can be conserved through the sacrifice of your own interests, be prepared to forfeit the advantage, but stand like a rock when God's truth is in balance.

F. B. MEYER, *Bible Commentary*

It is not by seeking more fertile regions where toil is lighter—happier circumstances free from difficult complications and troublesome people—but by bringing the high courage of a devout soul, clear in principle and aim, to bear upon what is given to us, that we brighten our inward light, lead something of a true life, and introduce the kingdom of heaven into the midst of our earthly day. If we cannot work out the will of God where God has placed us, then why has He placed us there?

JOHN HAMILTON THOM

A Forever Peace Prayer

And the smoke of the incense, which came with the prayers of the saints, ascended up before God out of the angel's hand.

Revelation 8:4 KJV

Author E. M. Bounds said, "Prayers are deathless. They outlive the lives of those who uttered them." It's true! Your prayers go up to heaven. There, angels hold golden bowls full of incense "which are the prayers of saints" (Revelation 5:8)! The prayers are then hurled back to earth, sprayed among God's people (Revelation 8:3–5). *All cries to God go full circle eternally and continually!*

Today's prayer of blessings for you, written by Saint Thérèse, is still alive! It's there for you to read, to take strength from, especially when you doubt where you are, where you're heading. Allow the saint's prayer to give you the peace you need. To trust you're exactly where God wants you. Take in her encouragement to hope, use your talents, pass on God's love, and live in contentment. Then bring yourself and your own prayers before God, settling into the reality of His presence and the foreverness of prayer.

365 Devotions on the Power of Prayer

May today there be peace within. May you trust God that you are exactly where you are meant to be. May you not forget the infinite possibilities that are born of faith. May you use those gifts that you have received, and pass on the love that has been given to you. May you be content knowing you are a child of God.

SAINT THÉRÈSE OF LISIEUX

Rest Assured

For I know the thoughts that I think toward you, saith the LORD, thoughts of peace, and not of evil, to give you an expected end. Then shall ye call upon me, and ye shall go and pray unto me, and I will hearken unto you. And ye shall seek me, and find me, when ye shall search for me with all your heart.

JEREMIAH 29:11–13 KJV

Nothing will happen today that God hasn't already seen coming. So rest assured that God's got you. That His constant thoughts toward you are filled with peace as He works out His plans for your life. Secure in that knowledge, you can have patience and be at peace no matter what your day brings. You and your life are in God's hands.

365 Devotions on the Power of Prayer

Here's a prayer to help you keep the peace:

I do not know, O God, what will happen to me today, I only know that nothing will happen to me but what has been foreseen by you from all eternity, and that is sufficient, O my God, to keep me in peace. I adore your eternal designs. I submit to them with all my heart. I desire them all and accept them all. I make a sacrifice of everything. I unite this sacrifice to that of your dear Son, my Saviour, begging you by His infinite merits, for the patience in troubles, and the perfect submission which is due to you in all that you will and design for me.

ÉLISABETH OF FRANCE

Peace Seekers

Blessed (happy, fortunate, to be envied) are they who keep His testimonies, and who seek, inquire for and of Him and crave Him with the whole heart. . . . Great peace have they who love Your law; nothing shall offend them or make them stumble.

PSALM 119:2, 165 AMPC

Resign every forbidden joy; restrain every wish that is not referred to His will; banish all eager desires, all anxiety. Desire only the will of God; seek Him alone, and you will find peace.

FRANÇOIS FÉNELON

Take no thought for tomorrow. Rest in [God's] Presence brings Peace. God will help you. Desire brings fulfillment. Peace like a quiet flowing river cleanses, sweeps all irritants away. You shall be taught, continue these prayer times, even if they seem fruitless. The devil will try by any means to stop them. Heed him not. He will say evil spirits may enter in. Heed him not. Rest your nerves. Tired nerves are a reflection on, not of, God's Power. Hope all the time. Do not be afraid of poverty. Let money flow freely. [God] will let it flow in, but you must let it flow out. [He] never send[s] money to stagnate—only to those who pass it on.

God Calling

Where Jesus is,
storms cease
and the sick are
made whole.

Where Storms Cease

[Jesus] said to them, "Come away by yourselves to a secluded place and rest a little while."

Mark 6:31 nasb

When the Apostles returned they had much to tell. Some were flushed with success, others radiant with victory over demons, others, perhaps, overstrained and weary, and all needing the quiet, holy influence of repose and silence in the Lord's company. And in those quiet hours or days, as the fever passed out of them, He taught them memorable lessons of how He would feed the world by His Church, and how His people would be safe amid the storms that swept the sea, for always He would watch them from the height, and come to them at the moment when His help was most needed.

Christ sits as host at the great table of the Church, and the meager resources of His servants yield the starting point for His multiplication of bread. He bids us go and consider how little we have, that we may properly estimate the greatness of His help. Notice how the upward look precedes the breaking and giving. There is enough for each, not of bread alone, but of fish; and the disciples are refreshed by another kind of ministry. So the Lord recreates us by turning exhausted energies into new channels. What threatens to overpower us brings Christ to our side. But His footsteps must be arrested, if we would have His company. Where Jesus is, storms cease and the sick are made whole.

F. B. Meyer, Bible Commentary

Confide in God

So Peter was kept in prison, but fervent prayer for him was persistently made to God by the church (assembly). The very night before Herod was about to bring him forth, Peter was sleeping between two soldiers, fastened with two chains, and sentries before the door were guarding the prison.

Acts 12:5–6 AMPC

The murderous King Herod was on a rampage. He'd already had James killed. Now Peter had been arrested and thrown into prison, likely to meet the same fate as James. Yet Peter didn't stay awake fearing what would happen on the morrow. Instead, he slept. Such was his faith in God, his assurance that the Lord would watch over him, keep him safe (Psalm 3:5; 4:8).

Peter was sleeping—Here is an instance of remarkable composure, and an illustration of the effects of peace of conscience and of confidence in God. It was doubtless known to Peter what the intention of Herod was. James had just been put to death, and Peter had no reason to expect a better fate. And yet in this state he slept as quietly as if there had been no danger, and it was necessary that he should be roused even by an angel to contemplate his condition and to make his escape. There is nothing that will give quiet rest and gentle sleep so certainly as a conscience void of offence; and in the midst of imminent dangers, he who confides in God may rest securely and calmly.

Barnes' Notes on the Bible

Peace of a Thankful Heart

Let the peace that comes from Christ rule in your hearts. For as members of one body you are called to live in peace. And always be thankful.

Colossians 3:15 NLT

Giving thanks to God brings out a myriad of benefits. An attitude of gratitude makes us happier, increases our psychological well-being, transforms emotions from negative to positive, strengthens relationships, gives us a more optimistic outlook, prompts us to increase our giving, and decreases our stress. But best of all, it reminds us how much God loves us, making our inner peace bubble up from within and spread without.

Gratitude consists in a watchful, minute attention to the particulars of our state, and to the multitude of God's gifts, taken one by one. It fills us with a consciousness that God loves and cares for us, even to the least event and smallest need of life. It is a blessed thought, that from our childhood God has been laying His fatherly hands upon us, and always in benediction; that even the strokes of His hands are blessings, and among the chiefest we have ever received. When this feeling is awakened, the heart beats with a pulse of thankfulness. Every gift has its return of praise. It awakens an unceasing daily converse with our Father—He speaking to us by the descent of blessings, we to Him by the ascent of thanksgiving. And all our whole life is thereby drawn under the light of His countenance, and is filled with a gladness, serenity, and peace which only thankful hearts can know.

Henry Edward Manning

Cultivating Calm

I've cultivated a quiet heart. Like a baby content in its mother's arms, my soul is a baby content.

PSALM 131:2 MSG

David, psalmist and king, had trained himself to trust God, to put all things in His hands. He saw God as a stable, ever-present, and powerful force for good and right in his life, looking for no other outside influence to rescue him. To firm that up within himself, he'd talk to his soul: "Wait calmly for God alone, my soul, because my hope comes from him. He alone is my rock and my savior—my stronghold. I cannot be shaken" (Psalm 62:5–6 GW).

You too can cultivate a quiet heart and calm soul by making God your sole rock and stronghold. Pray to Him and remind yourself that He alone can—and will—handle everything that comes your way.

Worry Less, Pray More

The cry of the child-heart. The psalmist. . .did not exercise himself. . .in things beyond his power, but left God to reveal them to him as he was able to receive them. . . . Clearly he had not reached this position without effort. He had found it necessary to still and quiet himself, as a nurse quiets a fretful babe. There had been a time when he was fed at the breast of the world's consolations. The weaning had been hard, but he had learned to get all from God and to draw on His sustaining grace.

F. B. MEYER, *Bible Commentary*

Your Burden Bearer

Blessed be the Lord, Who bears our burdens and carries us day by day, even the God Who is our salvation! Selah [pause, and calmly think of that]!

Psalm 68:19 AMPC

How blessed you are to have a God who loves you so much He will not only bear your burdens but will carry you! And not just once but every single day! Knowing and truly believing this, living as if it is true (which it is), gives you the peace of mind, heart, body, and spirit you need to live a fabulous life, free of worry! Yet the benefits don't stop there. Along with God bearing your load, He's decided you will be strong! Today give God your worries. Believe that He's carrying them—and you. Then enter your day in the strength He gives you.

Begin your morning by going to God and praying, "Lord, my worries have been weighing me down. Thank You so much for carrying them—and me—today and every day. Such knowledge gives me the strength I need."

Worry Less, Pray More

All is well. Wonderful things are happening. Do not limit God at all. He cares and provides. Uproot self—the channel-blocker. Do not plan ahead; the way will unfold step by step. Leave tomorrow's burden. Christ is the Great Burden Bearer. You cannot bear His load and He only expects you to carry a little day-share.

God Calling

The Lord Your Light

When I fall, I shall arise; when I sit in darkness, the Lord shall be a light to me.

MICAH 7:8 AMPC

Child of God, when you are lost, when you have fallen, when you are going through tough times, when you feel you are at the lowest of lows, even there, you can find God's strength and light. No matter how low you have fallen, there is One who will lift you up with His right hand. Simply lift up your face, your prayer, your praise, and He, the Sun of Righteousness (Malachi 4:2), will send His Spirit to comfort you, to help you find your way back to Him. He will direct you to His Word, which will act like a lamp to your feet (Psalm 119:105). There you will find the guidance you seek.

Yes, there may be some dark days, some turmoil, some low points. But you, woman, are a child of God. You are protected. No one can snatch you out of His hand (John 10:28–30). You are never out of His reach or hearing (Isaiah 59:1).

As a sister of Christ and a child of God, you can say to yourself each and every day, "When I fall, I shall arise; when I sit in darkness, the Lord shall be a light to me."

How oft a gleam of glory sent
Straight through the deepest, darkest night,
Has filled the soul with heavenly light,
With holy peace and sweet content.

ANONYMOUS

A Faithful Risk

"Go in peace."

LUKE 8:48 NLV

For twelve years a woman had an "issue of blood" (Matthew 9:20 KJV), making her unclean and outcast. She was weak, helpless, and poor because she'd spent all her money looking for a cure from doctors but got no relief. Her condition had gone from bad to worse.

She'd heard about Jesus and was determined to be healed. She told herself over and over again, "If I can just touch His robe, I'll be made well!" (Matthew 9:21 HCSB). Finally, she made her way to Jesus, reached out and touched His robe, and instantly felt her blood flow stop.

Jesus, knowing power had coursed out of Him, stopped and asked, "Who touched my robe?"

Finally, she fell down trembling before Him. She told her story. Then Jesus lovingly, gently, assured her: "Courage, daughter. You took a risk of faith, and now you're well" (Matthew 9:22 MSG).

Here we meet the only woman Jesus addressed as "daughter." Here, in a society where women were the silent majority, Jesus prompted a woman to publicly tell her tale. Here only, we read of Jesus feeling His power leaving Him.

Just as this story is unique, so is every woman. Each has a unique issue she's dealing with. Yet each female follower can take comfort and strength from the fact that she has a loving Savior who wants her to take a risk of faith, reach out, and tap into His healing peace and power, unafraid.

Unafraid

The Divine Injunction

Be careful for nothing; but in every thing by prayer and supplication with thanksgiving let your requests be made known unto God. And the peace of God, which passeth all understanding, shall keep your hearts and minds through Christ Jesus.

Philippians 4:6–7 KJV

We have one of the most important, far-reaching, peace-giving, necessary, and practical prayer possibilities in Paul's words in Philippians 4:6–7—prayer as a cure for undue care.

Ours is an anxious world, and ours is an anxious race. The caution of Paul is well addressed: "In nothing be anxious." This is the divine injunction, and that we might be able to live above anxiety and freed from undue care, "in every thing by prayer and supplication with thanksgiving let your requests be made known unto God." This is the divinely prescribed remedy for all anxious cares, for all worry, for all inward fretting. . . .

Prayer over everything can quiet every distraction, hush every anxiety, and lift every care from care-enslaved lives and from care-bewildered hearts. The prayer specific is the perfect cure for all ills of this character which belong to anxieties, cares, and worries. Only prayer in everything can drive dull care away, relieve unnecessary heart burdens, and save from the besetting sin of worrying over things which we cannot help. Only prayer can bring into the heart and mind the peace "which passeth all understanding," and keep mind and heart at ease, free from burdensome care.

E. M. Bounds

Portal to Peace

Behold, I stand at the door and knock; if anyone hears and listens to and heeds My voice and opens the door, I will come in to him and will eat with him, and he [will eat] with Me.

Revelation 3:20 AMPC

If you're looking for unsurpassable peace in your life, or moments of calm throughout your day, there is a way, a portal to entering into that place of quiet serenity.

Knocking on the door of your heart, soul, mind, and spirit is Jesus, your Lord and the Prince of Peace. He is standing there, just waiting for you to hear His knock, to listen to and heed His voice. That's His part. Yours is to open the door to Him. All you need to do is allow Him entrance, and He will come through that portal. He will come in and permeate your entire being. He will remind you that all is meant for your good. That there's no reason to be afraid. That He is there to calm you, love you, tend to you, heal you, and bless you.

Today, this morning, before your feet hit the floor, remember who is on the other side of your portal. Remember what awaits you there. Then allow Him entrance. And allow Him to remain there throughout your day and to stay with you into the night, as your head once more hits the pillow and His love lifts you up into dreamland.

Peace in the Presence of God

Be free from love of money [including greed, avarice, lust, and craving for earthly possessions] and be satisfied with your present [circumstances and with what you have]; for He [God] Himself has said, I will not in any way fail you nor give you up nor leave you without support. [I will] not, [I will] not, [I will] not in any degree leave you helpless nor forsake nor let [you] down (relax My hold on you)! [Assuredly not!]

Hebrews 13:5 AMPC

To gain true peace, don't put your faith in money. Simply be content, knowing wherever you are, whatever your circumstances, God is with you.

I cannot imagine how religious persons can live satisfied without the practice of the presence of God. For my part, I keep myself retired with Him in the fund or center of my soul as much as I can; and while I am so with Him I fear nothing, but the least turning from Him is insupportable.

This exercise does not much fatigue the body; it is, however, proper to deprive it sometimes, nay, often, of many little pleasures which are innocent and lawful, for God will not permit that a soul which desires to be devoted entirely to Him should take other pleasures than with Him: that is more than reasonable.

I do not say that therefore we must put any violent constraint upon ourselves. No, we must serve God in a holy freedom; we must do our business faithfully, without trouble or disquiet, recalling our mind to God mildly, and with tranquility, as often as we find it wandering from Him.

BROTHER LAWRENCE

The Hard Thing

Thou hast shewed thy people hard things.

PSALM 60:3 KJV

When hard times or difficult tasks come your way, don't lose your peace. Just know God will be with you, helping you do and get through the hard thing.

I have always been glad that the psalmist said to God that some things were hard. There is no mistake about it; there are hard things in life. Some beautiful pink flowers were given me this summer, and as I took them I said, "What are they?" And the answer came, "They are rock flowers; they grow and bloom only on rocks where you can see no soil." Then I thought of God's flowers growing in hard places; and I feel, somehow, that He may have a peculiar tenderness for His "rock flowers" that He may not have for His lilies and roses.

MARGARET BOTTOME

There will be no limit to what you can accomplish. Realize that. Never relinquish any task or give up the thought of any task because it seems beyond your power, only if you see it is not [God's] Will for you. This [He] command[s] you. Think of the tiny snowdrop-shoot in the hard ground. No certainty even that when it has forced its weary way up, sunlight and warmth will greet it. What a task beyond its power that must seem. But with the inner urge of Life within the seed compelling it, it carries out that task. The Kingdom of Heaven is like unto this.

God Calling

Spiritual Sowing

He who sows to his flesh will of the flesh reap corruption, but he who sows to the Spirit will of the Spirit reap everlasting life.

GALATIANS 6:8 NKJV

What are you sowing into your life?

When you're in a state of worry, you're sowing to your flesh, planting worry-seeds that will reap only more worry, or worse, grow into outright fear and panic. Before you know it, you're doing or saying something you didn't want to do or say, something that may destroy or deaden the spirits of others.

What you want to do is sow in the Spirit, not the flesh. So, when worry crops up—as it will do—take some deep breaths. Remember who created you and continues each day to re-create you. Dig into the Word. Find a verse that calms your spirit and builds up your faith. Write that verse upon your heart by memorizing it, making it part of your spiritual literacy. Then seek God's face and peace. Soon, you'll be sowing in the Spirit and reaping the light of eternal life.

If you need help getting there from here, consider praying a prayer like this: "I'm tired of sowing worry, Lord. It only grows up into bigger worries, or worse. Help me grow in You, sowing to the Spirit, reaping Your light."

Worry Less, Pray More

Life is a seedtime. It is the opportunity of preparing for heavenly harvests. The open furrows invite the seed, and every moment, in some form, we scatter seeds that we shall inevitably meet again in their fruition.

F. B. MEYER, *Bible Commentary*

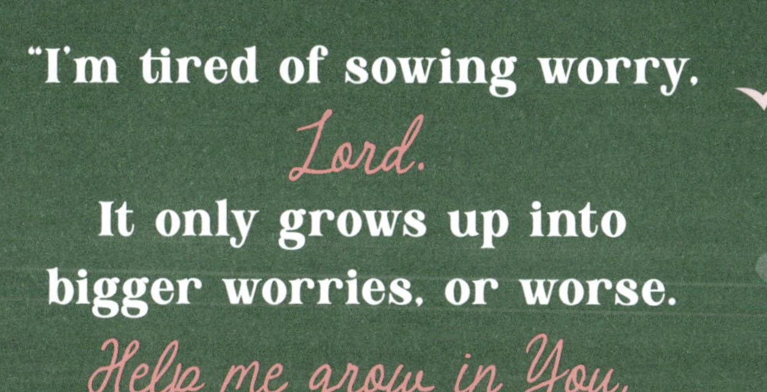

"I'm tired of sowing worry,
Lord.
It only grows up into
bigger worries, or worse.
Help me grow in You,
sowing to the Spirit,
reaping Your light."

A Conscious Peace

You shall not be afraid of the terror by night,
nor of the arrow that flies by day.

PSALM 91:5 NKJV

The deepest concerns of our souls, whether they be good or bad, are furthered during sleep. It is not merely a physical fact that you go to bed perplexed and wake clear-minded; God has been ministering to you during sleep. Sometimes God cannot get at us until we are asleep. In the Bible there are times when in the deep slumber of the body God has taken the souls of His servants into deeper communion with Himself (for example, Genesis 2:21; 15:12). Often when a problem or perplexity harasses the mind and there seems no solution, after a night's rest you find the solution easy, and the problem has no further perplexity. Think of the security of the saint in sleeping or in waking, "You shall not be afraid for the terror by night, nor of the arrow that flies by day." Sleep is God's celestial nurse who croons away our consciousness, and God deals with the unconscious life of the soul in places where only He and His angels have charge. As you retire to rest, give your soul and God a time together, and commit your life to God with a conscious peace for the hours of sleep, and deep and profound developments will go on in spirit, soul, and body by the kind, creating hand of our God.

OSWALD CHAMBERS, *Daily Thoughts for Disciples (September 19)*

Bearing Up

My strength and power are made perfect (fulfilled and completed) and [show themselves most effective in [your] weakness. Therefore, I will all the more gladly glory in my weaknesses and infirmities, that the strength and power of Christ (the Messiah) may rest (yes, may pitch a tent over and dwell) upon me!

2 Corinthians 12:9 AMPC

When we are so downcast and weak that we cannot lift our chins up off the floor, there is One who is joyfully waiting to ease our burden, to lift us up into the peace that we crave.

When you are more down than out, go to Jesus. Admit that your troubles have brought you to a place of weakness. Then watch Him and His glory and presence pitch a tent over you where He will infuse you with His strength so that you can bear up and rise again.

My strength is made perfect in weakness—That is, the strength which I impart to my people is more commonly and more completely manifested when my people feel that they are weak. It is not imparted to those who feel that they are strong and who do not realize their need of divine aid. It is not so completely manifested to those who are vigorous and strong as to the feeble. It is when we are conscious that we are feeble, and when we feel our need of aid, that the Redeemer manifests his power to uphold, and imparts his purest consolations.

Barnes' Notes on the Bible

In the Depths of Peace

You are all one in Christ.

GALATIANS 3:28 NKJV

The union of your soul with mine. . .is a union to which my heart fully responds, not in a way of emotional transport, but in the depths of peace; there is nothing of nature in it. It is a union in Jesus Christ. We are one in a sense of our lost condition, and one in self-abandonment. Oh! blessed oneness with Christ, where all evils perish; and there remains only the casualties inseparable from the state of humanity. How wonderful is this operation—the sacred mingling of a poor creature with its God, where all the evils of our fallen nature, are removed from the depths of the soul, and the soul, in its elemental being is lost in its original! There all the little ones are united in Him,—these little drops of water reassembled in the divine ocean! How swiftly do the streams embrace each other, and flow into one channel, when the obstructions are removed! When souls become pure in Jesus Christ, they flow into one another with the same rapidity. Purity of soul consists in an entire separation from self, and re-union with God. The soul *can* return to self; it has the power, and therefore is not infallible. . . .

It seems to me, that I am one with Him, and inseparable, and you are the same; and thus, we are one in Him, and one with each other.

MADAM GUYON

Waiting Quietly

It is good that one should hope in and wait quietly for the salvation (the safety and ease) of the Lord.

LAMENTATIONS 3:26 AMPC

Those who deal with God will find it is not in vain to trust Him; for, one, He is good to those who do. His tender mercies are over all His works; all His creatures taste of His goodness. But He is in a particular manner good to those who wait for Him. Note, while trouble is prolonged and deliverance is deferred, we must patiently wait for God and His gracious return to us.

While we wait for Him by faith, we must seek Him by prayer; our souls must seek Him, else we do not seek so as to find. Our seeking will help to keep up our waiting. To those who thus wait and seek, God will be gracious. He will show them His marvelous loving-kindness.

And, two, those who do so will find it good for them. It is good to hope and quietly wait for the salvation of the Lord; to hope that it will come, through the difficulties that lie in the way. To wait till it does come, though it be long delayed; and while we wait, to be quiet and silent, not quarreling with God, nor making ourselves uneasy.

If we call to mind, "Father, thy will be done," we may have hope that all will end well at last.

MATTHEW HENRY

Seek Silence

Be silent before the Lord God!

ZEPHANIAH 1:7 NASB

If your desire and aim is to reach the destination of the path and home of true happiness, of grace and glory by a straight and safe way, then earnestly apply your mind to seek constant purity of heart, clarity of mind, and calmness of the senses. Gather up your heart's desire and fix it continually on the Lord God above. To do so, you must withdraw yourself as far as you can from friends and from everyone else and from the activities that hinder you from such a purpose. Grasp every opportunity when you can find the place, time, and means to devote yourself to silence and contemplation and gathering the secret fruits of silence, so that you can escape the shipwreck of this present age and avoid the restless agitation of the noisy world.

Simplify your heart with all care, diligence, and effort so that, still and at peace, you can remain always in the Lord within, as if your mind were already in the now of eternity. In this way you will be able to commit yourself completely and fully to God in all difficulties and eventualities and be willing to submit yourself patiently to His will and good pleasure at all times.

There can be no greater happiness than to place one's all in Him who lacks nothing. Cast yourself, all of yourself, with confidence into God and He will sustain you, heal you, and make you safe.

ALBERT THE GREAT

A Very Blessed Thing

Jesus said to the woman, Your faith has saved you; go (enter) into peace [in freedom from all the distresses].

Luke 7:50 AMPC

When the many tears from her eyes fell upon His feet, He did not withdraw them. When those feet were wiped with the tresses of her hair, still He did not withdraw them; and when she ventured upon a yet closer familiarity and not only kissed His feet but did not cease to kiss them, He still did not withdraw them but quietly accepted all that she did. And when the precious ointment was poured in lavish abundance upon His precious feet, He did not chastise her; neither did He refuse her gifts but tacitly accepted them, although without a word of acknowledgement just then.

It is a very blessed thing for any one of us to be accepted before God, even though no word has come from His lips assuring you that you are. When your tears and cries and secret love and earnest seeking—when your confession of sin, your struggle after faith, and the beginning of your faith are just accepted by the Lord, although He has not yet said to you, "Your sins are forgiven," it is a very blessed stage for you to have reached, for the Lord does not begin to accept anyone and then draw back, even by a silence which seems constant. He accepted this woman's love and gifts, though for a time, He gave her no assurance of that acceptance, and that fact must have greatly encouraged her.

Charles Spurgeon

Daily Refill

O Lord, be gracious unto us; we have waited for thee: be thou their arm every morning, our salvation also in the time of trouble.

Isaiah 33:2 KJV

When you feel weak in your own power, when you're confused as to who you truly are, when you feel hopeless, that's the time to go to the One who never changes. Seek God, without whom you're powerless. Ask Him to take away all that's not of Him and to fill you with the fruits of His Spirit. Flee to the refuge that holds all promise for your life, trusting He'll bring you through. He'll renew you. As you wait on God, expect that He'll power you up. He'll be your arm of strength, your defense every morning, and help you meet whatever your day brings.

365 Devotions on the Power of Prayer

Pray:

O Lord, reassure me with Your quickening Spirit; without You I can do nothing. Mortify in me all ambition, vanity, vainglory, worldliness, pride, selfishness, and resistance from God, and fill me with love, peace, and all the fruits of the Spirit. O Lord, I know not what I am, but to You I flee for refuge. I would surrender myself to You, trusting Your precious promises and against hope believing in hope. You are the same yesterday, today, and forever; and therefore, waiting on Thee, Lord, I trust that I shall at length renew my strength.

WILLIAM WILBERFORCE

Slow and Steady

"Blessed be God, who has given peace to his people Israel just as he said he'd do. Not one of all those good and wonderful words that he spoke through Moses has misfired. May God, our very own God, continue to be with us just as he was with our ancestors—may he never give up and walk out on us. May he keep us centered and devoted to him, following the life path he has cleared, watching the signposts, walking at the pace and rhythms he laid down for our ancestors."

1 Kings 8:56–58 MSG

It's so easy to get caught up in the frenzy of the world and people around us. But people of God are to be walking in God's rhythm. When they do, miracles happen.

So today, set your pace and rhythm with God's—slow and steady.

Be still before [God]. How often in a crisis man rushes hither and thither. Rush is a sign of weakness. Quiet abiding is a sign of strength. A few quiet actions, as you are led to do them, and all is accomplished wisely and rightly, more quickly and more effectually than could be done by those who rush about and act feverishly. Guidance IS Guidance, the being led, the being shown the way. Believe this. Softly across life's tumult, comes the gentle Voice, "Peace, be still." The waves of difficulty will hear. They will fall back. There will be a great calm. And then the Still, Small Voice of Guidance.

God Calling

Quiet Retreat

You're my place of quiet retreat; I wait for your Word to renew me. . . . For those who love what you reveal, everything fits—no stumbling around in the dark for them.

Psalm 119:114, 165 msg

There is a place like no other. And that place is in God and His Word. There, amid all His words of wisdom, guidance, love, hope, and peace, you find a way to be renewed. You find worthy things to set your mind on. You find a place where your heart, spirit, and soul can be uplifted. And after spending time with God and His Word in that quiet place of retreat, you can look beyond and rise above the slights and insults, the arrows and the thorns of this world.

Yet the benefit of immersing yourself in God's Word does not end there. For it brings you to a place of love. So interested are you in the soothing balm, you cannot but want to linger there. The Word fills you with the guidance you need, the light that illuminates your way. It reveals as well as infuses you with all the love you can possibly hold, extinguishing in your heart all the unseemly passions.

Today, before you do anything, go on that retreat into God's Word. In the silence, allow it to renew your entire being. And as you rise, do so in peace of mind, heart, spirit, and soul, knowing God has you covered.

The Peace We Seek

We have a building from God, a house not made with hands, eternal in the heavens.

2 Corinthians 5:1 NKJV

A father. . .had lost his little boy. Adding to his great pain was the fact that he had not thought much about the future because he was so taken up with this world and its affairs. When that little boy, his only son, died, that father's heart was broken, and every night when he got home from work, he could be found with his yellowed tallow candle and his family Bible in his room. He was hunting up all that he could find there about heaven. When someone asked him what he was doing, the father replied, "I am trying to find out where my boy has gone. I need to know."

This story reflects man's interest in the afterlife. Some call it an undiscovered country from where no traveler returns. But the hope of every Christian is the place called heaven—a better country. While men constantly seek to find some better place, some lovelier place than we have now, Christians have this hope. They don't look down to this earth, but they lift their eyes.

My friends, let us believe this good old Book, that our hope is based on the fact that heaven is not a myth. Let us be prepared to follow dear ones who have gone before.

There, and there alone, can we find the peace we seek for.

Dwight L. Moody

Do not look forward
to the changes and chances
of this life in fear;
rather look to them with
full hope that, as they
arise, God, whose you are,
will deliver you out of them.

God's Firm Grip

"I, your GOD, have a firm grip on you and I'm not letting go. I'm telling you, 'Don't panic. I'm right here to help you.'"

ISAIAH 41:13 MSG

One of the first things a child learns is to hold a parent's hand when crossing the street. Yet that's also one of the first things a child wants to *stop* doing when she considers herself "not a baby anymore." How ironic that we have to learn that lesson all over again when we are neither a baby nor a girl but a woman fully grown, one who needs Father God's hand to hold and sometimes to be carried as well.

Do not look forward to the changes and chances of this life in fear; rather look to them with full hope that, as they arise, God, whose you are, will deliver you out of them. He has kept you hitherto—do you but hold fast to His dear hand, and He will lead you safely through all things; and, when you cannot stand, He will bear you in His arms. Do not look forward to what may happen tomorrow; the same everlasting Father who cares for you today, will take care of you tomorrow, and every day. Either He will shield you from suffering, or He will give you unfailing strength to bear it. Be at peace then, and put aside all anxious thoughts and imaginations.

FRANCIS DE SALES

Becoming a Prayer Carrier

Pray all the time; thank God no matter what happens. This is the way God wants you who belong to Christ Jesus to live. Don't suppress the Spirit.

1 Thessalonians 5:17–19 msg

There's a reason we are encouraged to pray without ceasing: It's the one and only pathway to peace. It is those niggling things, those thoughts, that tear us and others down. They are the greatest of peace disruptors.

Instead of allowing your shortcomings to submarine your calm and joy, carry prayer into everything you do—washing dishes, making meals, walking the dog, listening to the news. Pray unceasingly in the Spirit. And peace will be yours.

Do not be discouraged at your faults; bear with yourself in correcting them, as you would with your neighbor. Lay aside this ardor of mind, which exhausts your body, and leads you to commit errors. Accustom yourself gradually to carry prayer into all your daily occupations. Speak, move, work, in peace, as if you were in prayer, as indeed you ought to be. Do everything without excitement, by the spirit of grace. As soon as you perceive your natural impetuosity gliding in, retire quietly within, where is the kingdom of God. Listen to the leadings of grace, then say and do nothing but what the Holy Spirit shall put in your heart. You will find that you will become more tranquil, that your words will be fewer and more effectual, and that, with less effort, you will accomplish more good.

François Fénelon

For Such a Time

"If you keep silent at this time, relief and deliverance will rise for the Jews from another place, but you and your father's house will perish. And who knows whether you have not come to the kingdom for such a time as this?"

ESTHER 4:14 ESV

Upon discovering the king of Persia's edict announcing a day when all Jews—young and old, women and children—would be destroyed in the kingdom, Mordecai tore his clothes and went into deep mourning.

Hearing of her cousin's grief, Queen Esther herself became deeply distressed. She sent one of the king's eunuchs to go to Mordecai to discover what'd happened. Mordecai sent word back to Esther, telling her that this may be her time to talk to the king and ask for his help to save her people. Perhaps this was why, through God's providence, she had become queen in the first place.

After receiving his message, a resolved Esther told Mordecai to ask her people to fast and pray for three days, saying, "Then I will go to the king, though it is against the law, and if I perish, I perish" (Esther 4:16 ESV).

Perhaps you feel God is calling you, willing you to be brave in His name. If so, pray. Ask God to replace your worries with His peace, to replace your fears with His courage, to replace your weakness with His strength. Don't miss this opportunity to serve God at such a time as this.

Worry Less, Pray More

Heart Ease

My desire is to have you free from all anxiety and distressing care. . . . Therefore humble yourselves. . . , casting the whole of your care [all your anxieties, all your worries, all your concerns, once and for all] on Him, for He cares for you affectionately and cares about you watchfully. . . . Fret not yourself—it tends only to evildoing.

1 Corinthians 7:32; 1 Peter 5:6–7; Psalm 37:8 AMPC

How many times have you had a worry or concern and given it to God in prayer, only to take it up again the next day?

God's desire is for you to not worry, be anxious, or fret—about anything! Ever! He wants you to give Him all your burdens—and then walk away! Don't look back! Why? Because worrying about things only stirs up more pain.

Today, follow God's desires. Place all burdens at God's feet and pick up His love for you.

Paul in writing to the Corinthians says, "I would have you without carefulness" (1 Corinthians 7:32), and this is the will of God. Prayer has the ability to do this very thing. "Casting all your care upon him; for he careth for you," is the way Peter puts it in 1 Peter 5:7; while Psalm 37:8 says, "Fret not thyself in any wise to do evil." Oh, the blessedness of a heart at ease from all inward care, exempt from undue anxiety, in the enjoyment of the peace of God which passeth all understanding!

E. M. Bounds

The Comfort of God's Name

We will walk in the name of the LORD our God for ever and ever.

MICAH 4:5 KJV

Sometimes you may find your eyes glazing over at the name God. Perhaps, because it's used so often in your prayers, it's lost its power for you. If so, consider using a name the Hebrews used for Him, one that reflects His many aspects, one that sparks your heart and fits your current need. When the slave Hagar was running away from her mistress, Sarah, God found her in the desert, then spoke to, encouraged, and instructed her. There she referred to Him as the God Who Watches Over Me. You too can address God by His many aspects by referring to Him as the Lord Is There, the Lord Is My Shepherd, the Lord Will Provide, Strong Tower, God Most High, Refuge, Shield, Fortress, the Lord Is Peace, the Lord My Rock, or Dwelling Place. Call God by the name your heart needs to bring more power to your prayer and life!

365 Devotions on the Power of Prayer

God, this word we call you by is almost dead and meaningless, transient and empty like all the words men use. We ask you to renew its force and meaning, to make it once again a name that brings your promise to us. Make it a living word which tells us that you will be for us as you have always been—trustworthy and hidden and very close to us, Our God, now and for ever.

HUUB OOSTERHUIS

Rest vs. Stress

Stand by the roads and look; and ask for the eternal paths, where the good, old way is; then walk in it, and you will find rest for your souls. But they said, We will not walk in it!

JEREMIAH 6:16 AMPC

Have a decision to make? A path to choose? Looking for direction? For peace? God has all the answers for you and even outlines them in Jeremiah 6:16. Step 1: Stand where you are and look around. Consider all the possible options. Step 2: Pray. Ask God for His good way. Step 3: Walk in it. Now that you know the right way (via prayer, heeding God's voice, and using the Bible as your road map), you will find rest for your souls.

Your other choice is to (a) do none of those things or (b) refuse to walk in the path God has laid out for you. Both lead to stress.

So stop. Stand by, now, in this moment. Take steps 1 through 3. Choose rest, not stress.

Stress Less, Pray More

There is rest and peace enjoyed in the ways of God, and in the ordinances of the Gospel; wisdom's ways are ways of peace, which are the lesser paths; and in the doctrines of the Gospel, when the heart is established with them, the mind is tranquil and serene, and at rest, which before was fluctuating and wavering, and tossed to and fro with every wind; but the principal rest is in Christ himself.

Gill's Exposition of the Bible

Hope over Discouragement

Why are you cast down, O my soul? And why are you disquieted within me? Hope in God; for I shall yet praise Him, the help of my countenance and my God.

PSALM 42:11 NKJV

If I am asked how we are to get rid of discouragement, I can only say. . .we must give it up. It is never worthwhile to argue against discouragement. There is only one argument that can meet it, and that is the argument of God.

When David was in the midst of what were perhaps the most discouraging moments of his life, he found his city burned and his wives stolen. He and his men wept together until they had no more power to weep; and when his men, exasperated at their misfortunes, spoke of stoning him, then we are told, "But David encouraged himself in the Lord his God." The result was a magnificent victory in which all that they had lost was more than restored to them. This always will be, and always must be, the result of a courageous faith, because faith lays hold of the omnipotence of God.

The psalmist does not analyze his disquietude or try to argue it away, but he turns at once to the Lord. Then by faith David began to praise his Lord. It was the only way. Discouragement flies where faith appears. And in the same way, faith flies when discouragement appears. We must choose between them, for they will not be mixed.

HANNAH WHITALL SMITH

Truly Home

"When he was still a great way off, his father saw him and had compassion, and ran and fell on his neck and kissed him."

LUKE 15:20 NKJV

God knows there may be times when we wander off our path. But there's comfort knowing He will be there to receive us when we come to ourselves and make our way back to Him, seeking peace, help, love. Then, in that moment when, downhearted, we step once more into His arms, we witness His compassion for us. We feel His tenderness. And we know we're truly home, never to roam, forever to cling to the One who lifts and mends our heavy hearts.

Too often we desire God's gifts apart from Himself. The *far country* [Luke 15:13 KJV] is not far in actual distance, but in the alienation of the heart. You may be living in a pious home and yet be in the *far country*.

The first step to God is to come to ourselves. The prodigal's real nature stood face to face with the ruin and havoc of his sin. Never, for a moment, had the Father ceased to love and yearn. There was an instant response to the slightest indication of repentance. Love was quicker than words, to understand what the prodigal meant. The confession was therefore cut short. Note the profuse welcome, meeting every need—the robe of righteousness, the ring of reconciliation, the kiss of love, the shoes of a holy walk, the feast of fellowship.

F. B. MEYER, *Bible Commentary*

King of Peace

But I see another law in my members, warring against the law of my mind, and bringing me into captivity to the law of sin which is in my members. . . . Who shall deliver me from the body of this death? I thank God through Jesus Christ our Lord. So then with the mind I myself serve the law of God; but with the flesh the law of sin.

Romans 7:23–25 KJV

Your character is determined by what you allow to reign over you. Is Christ on the throne of your life, thoughts, and spirit, or has something else taken possession of you, leading you down the wrong path? Although you may have no power to resist the thoughts that war against the law of your mind, Christ does. So call Him in! Invite the King of Peace to take over the throne of your mind once again. He will deliver you!

365 Devotions on the Power of Prayer

O Lord, come quickly and reign on Thy throne, for now ofttimes something rises up within me, and tries to take possession of Thy throne: pride, covetousness, uncleanness, and sloth want to be my kings; and then evil-speaking, anger, hatred, and the whole train of vices join with me in warring against myself, and try to reign over me. I resist them, I cry out against them, and say, "I have no other king than Christ." O King of Peace, come and reign in me, for I will have no king but Thee! Amen.

SAINT BERNARD

From Prayer to Peace

Rejoice evermore. Pray without ceasing. In every thing give thanks: for this is the will of God in Christ Jesus concerning you.

1 THESSALONIANS 5:16–18 KJV

How are we to let our moderation, our mildness, and our gentleness be universally and always known? We resolve to be benign and gentle. We remember the nearness of the Lord, but still we are hasty, quick, hard, and salty. We listen to the divine charge, "Be careful for nothing," yet still we are anxious, careworn, care-eaten, and care-tossed. How can we fulfill the divine word, so sweet and so large in promise, so beautiful in the eye, and yet so far from being realized? How can we enter upon the rich patrimony of being true, honest, just, and pure, and possess lovely things? The recipe is infallible, the remedy is universal, and the cure is unfailing. It is found in the words which we have so often herein referred to of Paul: "Be careful for nothing; but in every thing by prayer and supplication with thanksgiving let your requests be made known unto God" (Philippians 4:6).

This joyous, carefree, peaceful experience bringing the believer into a joyousness, living simply by faith day by day, is the will of God. . . . Not only is it God's will that we should find full deliverance from all care and undue anxiety, but He has ordained prayer as the means by which we can reach that happy state of heart.

E. M. BOUNDS

The Peace of Divine Guidance: Part 1

"I know the plans I have for you," declares the LORD, "plans to prosper you and not to harm you, plans to give you hope and a future."

JEREMIAH 29:11 NIV

When I was a child, my grandmother gave me a worry stone. Holding this flat, oval-shaped, polished gemstone between her fingers and thumb, Grandma showed me how to rub the stone. She said that when I did, I would gain relief from the concerns that plagued me.

As I grew, I used this worry stone when plagued by what-ifs. "What if I flunk this exam?" *Rub, rub. . .* I got a B. "What if Daddy should die?" *Rub, rub. . .* My father died on my sixteenth birthday. "What if Mark breaks up with me?" *Rub, rub. . . I* broke up with Mark.

As time went by, I realized it didn't matter how much I used the worry stone because it changed neither the present nor the future. So, I put the stone away but kept the worries close at hand.

Years later, I visited the only church in my town. There, for the first time, I connected with God in a personal, life-changing way. I began attending church and Sunday school every week and diving into God's Word with an unquenchable thirst.

As I read, I discovered the powerful words of Jeremiah 29:11–12. And my heart, which overcame all worry, overflowed with peace.

Power Prayers to Start Your Day

The Peace of Divine Guidance: Part 2

"You meant evil against me; but God meant it for good, in order to bring it about as it is this day, to save many people alive."

GENESIS 50:20 NKJV

God had plans for me! *Me!* I began to revel in this knowledge. I realized that when worries begin to rub at me, all I have to do is call upon Him, seek Him with all my heart, and tell Him all my fears of the future. He will listen and then lead me to go in the power of His divine guidance, urging me to be confident that He is before me in the going. He's got a plan for my life, full of hope in and prosperity with Him, and He will give me the power to proceed!

As I looked back on my past, I realized my dad's death had not been some sort of awful punishment for the sins of my life but a part of God's ultimate *plan*. God intends that everything that happens to us—good and bad—further His purposes for the ultimate good (Genesis 50:19–20). And although I'd lost my earthly father, I now knew I would never lose my heavenly Father.

If only Grandma had given me the gift of the Word instead of a worry stone! How much easier it would have been to cope with my fears of the future and my sense of trouble in the present.

Power Prayers to Start Your Day

The Peace of Divine Guidance: Part 3

The LORD *will go before you.*

ISAIAH 52:12 NIV

How many years I had wasted in the pit of despair over what-ifs, girded only with a tool like a worry stone instead of God's Word.

When worries about the future plague you, delve into God's Word, turn your heart to seek His face, and pray to the Lord your Savior who never ceases to "instruct you and teach you in the way you should go" and "guide you with [His] eye" (Psalm 32:8 NKJV). Ask God to give you the power of His divine guidance, helping you fulfill His plan for your life. And remember that "the LORD will go before you; and the God of Israel will be your reward" (Isaiah 52:12 KJV). He knows, sees, and appears in your future ahead of you. Thus you can leave the past you can never change or repair in His hands and walk into the future in rhythm with Him.

Today and every day, make and keep an appointment with your God. Allow His voice, His guidance, His peace, His strength, and His comfort to not just fill you up but grow you up.

Before your feet hit the floor, remind yourself, in the words of Saint Patrick, "I arise today, through. . .God's eye to look before me."

Power Prayers to Start Your Day

The Father Is Nearer

The disciples went and woke him, saying, "Lord, save us! We're going to drown!" He replied, "You of little faith, why are you so afraid?" Then he got up and rebuked the winds and the waves, and it was completely calm. The men were amazed and asked, "What kind of man is this? Even the winds and the waves obey him!"

MATTHEW 8:25–27 NIV

Sometimes storms come up out of nowhere. And before we know it, we're being rocked to and fro, unable to get control over the things that are besetting us. And that's the last thing we want—to not be in control. Our hearts start racing, palms begin sweating, and hopes commence circling the drain. We forget who is truly in control, who is riding the waves with us: the Lord and Father of all. But once we realize the Master is in the boat with us, all we have to do is sink into His arms and let Him take the helm, knowing we couldn't be in a safer place than His presence.

Storms must sweep all over our lives. The Master's sleep indicates the peace and security of his nature. What a contrast between our impatience and his infinite serenity! Our Lord was sure that the Father was with him (John 8:29). Near though the enemy may be, the Father is nearer. The everlasting arms are beneath you. You are beset behind and before, but no boat can sink when Christ is on board.

F. B. MEYER, *Bible Commentary*

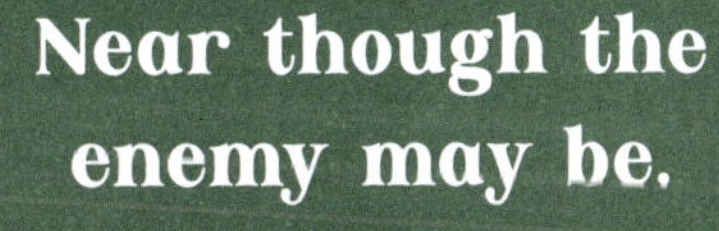

Near though the enemy may be,

the Father is nearer.

The everlasting arms are beneath you. You are beset behind and before, but no boat can sink when

Christ is on board.

A New Song

I waited patiently and expectantly for the Lord; and He inclined to me and heard my cry. He drew me up out of a horrible pit. . . . He has put a new song in my mouth, a song of praise to our God.

Psalm 40:1–3 AMPC

When God created woman, He made her a passionate, nurturing, caring being. As such, she is prone to stoically carrying the weight of others, especially loved ones, upon her own small shoulders. Fortunately, God, keenly aware of this predilection, provided her with a consolation prize—the gift of prayer.

When the faithful female meets her Creator via the vehicle of prayer, she's lifted up out of the earthen pit. In blessed spiritual communion with her Lord, she finds her faith, hope, love, and joy cannot help but increase. As the last chords of her wails of woe leave her lips, she is impelled to sing songs of celebration, thanking and praising God for all He has done, is doing, and will do. An overwhelming peace springs up within, for prayer has reminded her this earthly existence is merely a temporary state. One day, she'll be called homeward to live with her Father forever in mansions of glory. But for now, she's comforted knowing prayer is the consolation prize between this world and the next, and will forever be a privilege and spirit booster to all who wholeheartedly rely on their Creator.

Sweet Hour of Prayer

The Prayer of Silent Faith

Pray at all times (on every occasion, in every season) in the Spirit, with all [manner of] prayer and entreaty. To that end keep alert and watch with strong purpose and perseverance.

EPHESIANS 6:18 AMPC

Imagine a soul so closely united to God that it has no need of outward acts to remain attentive to the inward prayer. In these moments of silence and peace when it pays no heed to what is happening within itself, it prays and prays excellently, with a simple and direct prayer that God will understand perfectly by the action of grace.

The heart will be full of aspirations toward God without any clear expression. If it is the heart that prays, it is evident that sometimes and even continuously, it can pray by itself without any help from words, spoken or not. Here is something that few people understand. Though prayers may elude our own consciousness, they will not escape the consciousness of God.

This prayer, so empty of all images and perceptions, apparently so passive and yet so active, is—so far as the limitations of this life allow—pure adoration in spirit and in truth. It is adoration fully worthy of God in which the soul is united to Him as its ground, the created intelligence to the uncreated, without anything but a very simple attention of the mind and an equally simple application of the will. This is what is called the prayer of silent or of quiet or of bare faith.

JEAN-NICHOLAS GROU

Deep Peace in Reach

There has never been the slightest doubt in my mind that the God who started this great work in you would keep at it and bring it to a flourishing finish on the very day Christ Jesus appears.

PHILIPPIANS 1:6 MSG

The joy of the Lord in the spirit springs from an assurance that all the future, whatever it may be, is guaranteed by divine goodness, that being children of God, the love of God toward us is not of a mutable character, but abides and remains unchangeable. The believer feels an entire sanctification in leaving himself in the hands of eternal and immutable love. However happy I may be today, if I am in doubt concerning tomorrow, something is eating at the root of my peace; although the past may now be sweet in retrospect and the present fair in enjoyment, yet if the future be grim with fear, my joy is not mine, and deep peace is still out of my reach.

But when I know that He whom I have rested in has power and grace enough to complete that which He has begun in me and for me; when I see the work of Christ to be no halfway redemption, but a complete and eternal salvation; when I perceive that the promises are established upon an unchangeable basis and are in Christ Jesus, ratified by oath and sealed by blood, then my soul hath perfect contentment.

CHARLES SPURGEON

At All Times!

Pray at all times.

EPHESIANS 6:18 NASB

Pray at all times. Who can do this? How can we do it when we are surrounded by the cares of daily life? How can a mother love her child at all times? I can breathe and feel and hear at all times because all these are the functions of a healthy, natural life. If our spiritual life is healthy, under the power of the Holy Spirit, praying at all times will be natural.

Pray at all times. Does it refer to continual acts of prayer, in which we are to persevere until we receive an answer, or to the spirit of prayerfulness that should animate us all day? It includes both. Jesus gives us an example of this. We have to spend special times of prayer in private. We are also to walk all day in God's presence with our focus on heavenly things. Without set times of prayer, the spirit of prayer will be dull. Without the continual prayerfulness, the set times will not be effective.

Pray at all times. Does it refer to prayer for ourselves or for others? It refers to both, but too often we confine it to ourselves. The death of Christ brought Him to the place of everlasting intercession. Our death with Him to sin and self sets us free from selfishness and elevates us to the dignity of intercessor—one who can get life and blessing from God for others.

ANDREW MURRAY

Never Shaken

I will bless the LORD who guides me; even at night my heart instructs me. I know the LORD is always with me. I will not be shaken, for he is right beside me.

PSALM 16:7–8 NLT

These days, lots of businesses are open 24-7. But God has been open and available to His people day and night since they were created. So if you have the all-powerful Creator constantly by your side, guiding you in the day and advising you in the night, whatever could you be worried about?

Woman, make up your mind to see things through God's eternal perspective. Remember that your days are like a moment to Him. So live life to the fullest with no worries, fears, or anxieties to distract you or to keep you from the joy and peace that is yours in Christ.

God is with you. You will never be shaken. Let that stir your spirit into moving in rhythm with Him, filled with courage, peace, and joy, all the days of your life.

Worry Less, Pray More

No man or company of men, no power in earth or heaven can touch that soul which is abiding in Christ without first passing through His encircling presence and receiving the seal of His permission. If God be for us, it matters not who may be against us; nothing can disturb or harm us except He shall see that it is best for us and shall stand aside to let it pass.

HANNAH WHITALL SMITH

Angels' Charge

Because God's your refuge, the High God your very own home, evil can't get close to you. . . . He ordered his angels to guard you wherever you go. If you stumble, they'll catch you; their job is to keep you from falling.

Psalm 91:9–12 msg

In this world, it's easy to lose your peace unless you've built up an unshakable trust in God, believing He has everything under control. That's the kind of trust and faith worth pursuing.

[Rev. John Fletcher] would often say, "It is my business in all events to hang upon the Lord, with a sure trust and confidence, that He will order all things in the best time and manner. Indeed, it would be nothing to be a believer; nay, in truth, there would be no room for faith if everything were seen here. But against hope to believe in hope, to have a full confidence in that unseen power which so mightily supports us in all our dangers and difficulties—this is the believing which is acceptable to God."

Sometimes when I have expressed some apprehension of an approaching trial, he would answer, "I do not doubt but the Lord orders all; therefore I leave everything to Him." In outward dangers, if they were ever so great, he seemed to know no shadow of fear. When I was speaking once, concerning a danger to which we were then particularly exposed, he answered, "I know God always gives His angels charge concerning us; therefore we are equally safe everywhere."

CHARLES WESLEY

God's Blessing

The Lord bless you and watch, guard, and keep you;
the Lord make His face to shine upon and enlighten you
and be gracious (kind, merciful, and giving favor) to you;
the Lord lift up His [approving] countenance upon you and
give you peace (tranquility of heart and life continually).

Numbers 6:24–26 AMPC

When you feel as if the world is against you, when you feel as if you are all alone in this world, when you feel as if you have entered a darkness from which you cannot escape, when you feel peace is not just out of reach but nonexistent, pick up your copy of God's Word and home in on the passage above. For your feelings are often fiction, whereas your Bible is based on fact.

To reap all God offers you in this world, to become the woman He has created you to be, your feelings must be replaced with faith. Proverbs, the Bible book of wisdom, tells you that "he who leans on, trusts in, and is confident of his own mind and heart is a [self-confident] fool, but he who walks in skillful and godly Wisdom shall be delivered" (Proverbs 28:26 AMPC).

In other words, if you want peace of mind and heart, if you want to reap the richness of all God offers you—His blessing, protection, provision, light, grace, kindness, and calm—tap into the power and truth of the blessings in today's verses. In doing so, you will gain not only the peace for which you pine but the light for the way there.

"All Will Be Well"

And she called to her husband and said, Send me one of the servants and one of the donkeys, that I may go quickly to the man of God and come back again. And he said, Why go to him today? It is neither the New Moon nor the Sabbath. And she said, It will be all right.

2 Kings 4:22–23 AMPC

The things that happen in our lives, things over which we have no control, can easily and mightily disrupt our peace. But the power of such disruptions can and will abate when we call to mind our good God and those under His command and when we, with confidence, remind others and ourselves that "all will be well."

When a child is taken sick, it is the mother who is the best comforter; but there are limits to a mother's power to help. This woman of Shunem must be referred to in Hebrews 11:35. She was so sure of the life-restoring prayers of the great prophet that she did not feel it necessary to tell her husband what had befallen their son. Why should she grieve him, when the child would soon be given back to them! In noble confidence she dared to say that all would be well, and God did not disappoint nor fail. Shunem was fifteen miles from Carmel, and there was not an inch of the road which was not covered by the mother's splendid faith that God would make all-grace abound toward her.

F. B. MEYER, *Bible Commentary*

At the Master's Feet

Mary. . .seated herself at the Lord's feet
and was listening to His teaching.
LUKE 10:39 AMPC

The more we worry, the less we pray. And the less we pray, the more we worry. It's a vicious cycle. And the way to break it is to pray—not just by saying the same old prayer over and over. Or reading the same old devotional. Or repeating the same old psalm. Instead, begin exploring. Look around for some new ideas, words, books, verses. Better yet, consider spending some quiet moments with God, listening.

Chances are, you gift a lot of people with your time, sometimes more than you have to spare. But how much of your time are you gifting to God?

Before you get into your day, take stock and stop. Imagine yourself at Jesus' feet.

To do such imagining, you'll have to set down your phone. Step away from your computer or TV. Then, find a quiet place to which you can retreat and forget about all the to-dos you need to get done. Lean back into Jesus' presence. Listen to Him with both ears. Gift Him and yourself with those precious moments. When you do, He will gift you with that unsurpassing peace of mind, body, heart, spirit, and soul.

Stress Less, Pray More

Martha is active and conspicuous in serving; Mary, meditative and emotional, pouring her whole soul into one act of love.

Ellicott's Commentary for English Readers

Seeking Calm

May the God of your hope so fill you with all joy and peace in believing [through the experience of your faith] that by the power of the Holy Spirit you may abound and be overflowing (bubbling over) with hope.

Romans 15:13 AMPC

Hope, joy, and peace, form a triad which represents the attitude of the Christian in looking towards the future, and so far as that future is reflected on the present. Hope may be taken as including the other two, as it is upon the certainty of the Messianic promises that they all depend, just as it is through the constant energising power of the Holy Ghost that they are kept alive.

Ellicott's Commentary for English Readers

Every morning compose your soul for a tranquil day, and all through it be careful often to recall your resolution, and bring yourself back to it, so to say. If something discomposes you, do not be upset, or troubled; but having discovered the fact, humble yourself gently before God, and try to bring your mind into a quiet attitude. Say to yourself, "Well, I have made a false step; now I must go more carefully and watchfully." Do this each time, however frequently you fall. When you are at peace, use it profitably, making constant acts of meekness, and seeking to be calm even in the most trifling things. Above all, do not be discouraged; be patient; wait; strive to attain a calm, gentle spirit.

FRANCIS DE SALES

You Choose

[Jesus said,] "I have told you these things, so that in me you may have peace. In this world you will have trouble. But take heart! I have overcome the world."

John 16:33 NIV

According to the Bible, there are two kinds of happiness. The first is contingent upon what is happening around us, what our circumstances are. In other words, if things in our earthly existence are going well, we are happy. But there is an even deeper happiness for Christians—one that is based on the calm assurance that in spite of what is happening around us, we are trusting in Jesus, certain that the Holy Spirit is with us and that God will work all things out for our good. It's about rising above the trials and tribulations of this life to find that unspeakable happiness, that calmness, that sweet assurance in knowing that through flood and fire, through dirty diapers and dented fenders, through curfews and crying jags, the Lord's light is upon us, shining through us, exuding a peace others are attracted to and yearn to possess.

Yes, woman of the Way, you have the choice to be joyful or fearful, to hand your troubles over to Jesus or keep them firmly in your white-knuckled grip, to feel a growing hopelessness and desperation or feed a deep sense of peace. It is an option you choose to take each and every moment of every day, regardless of your circumstances.

Mother's Secret of a Happy Life

. . .you have the choice to be

joyful or fearful,

to hand your troubles over to Jesus or keep them firmly in your white-knuckled grip, to feel a growing hopelessness and desperation or

feed a deep sense of peace.

Expect Peace

Blessed (happy, fortunate, to be envied) are all those who [earnestly] wait for Him, who expect and look and long for Him [for His victory, His favor, His love, His peace, His joy, and His matchless, unbroken companionship]!

ISAIAH 30:18 AMPC

In all things you have before you today, look for God. Look for His peace. Expect it to enter into your day, to lead you in its light, to be a pulsating presence that meets you wherever you turn. Imagine God being by your side in the morning as you get ready for the day. Know He is standing closer than you could ever believe or expect, waiting to help and heal you with His peace and love.

One great sign of the practical recognition of the "divine moment," and of our finding God's habitation in it, is constant calmness and peace of mind. Events and things come with the moment; but God comes with them, too. So that if He comes in the sunshine, we find rest and joy; and if He comes in the storm, we know He is King of the storms, and our hearts are not troubled. God Himself, though possessing a heart filled with the tenderest feelings, is, nevertheless, an everlasting tranquillity; and when we enter into His holy tabernacle, our souls necessarily enter into the tabernacle of rest.

THOMAS COGSWELL UPHAM

The Hidden Life

[As far as this world is concerned] you have died, and your [new, real] life is hidden with Christ in God.

Colossians 3:3 AMPC

The so-called higher Christian life is. . .one of continual rest in Jesus, of peace that surpasses all understanding. It's calm assurance and abundant joy in the midst of trials and chaos.

But how do we live out this higher life? The key is obtaining childlike trust and faith in God, knowing that through thick and thin, He is with us and *wants* to carry our burdens. After all, Jesus has already taken on the burden of our sins. What makes us think we have to carry the load of our worries, woes, and cares about the present—and sometimes future—upon our own inadequate shoulders?

Most of us hesitate to give God our burdens because we're not sure He can handle them. . . . It's as if *He* is the child and *we* are the father, always knowing what's best. That is a ludicrously fantastic role reversal when the fact of the matter is that *we* are the children and *God* is the Father—the Father who *always* knows best. . . .

We must train our minds and hearts to believe what the hymn writer Fanny Crosby, who was blind, understood: "For I know that whate'er befall me, Jesus doeth all things well"! Notice her use of the present tense—"doeth." He is with you now, waiting to carry your load. To turn your trial into triumph!

Woman's Secret of a Happy Life

Keep Calm and Carry On

"When reports come in of wars and rumored wars, keep your head and don't panic. This is routine history; this is no sign of the end."

MATTHEW 24:6 MSG

These days, just reading or listening to the news can be a major stressor. For you hear not only of wars between nations but within nations. Then there are the wars on drugs, sex trafficking, opioid addiction, insurrections, pandemics, etc. It's enough to discourage and dishearten even the most stoic of listeners, draining our compassion, making us feel helpless, and leaving us wondering, *How, oh how can I fix this?*

Yet Jesus tells you not to worry or panic. To keep your head. That this is just how it is. Meanwhile, what are you to do to keep calm and carry on?

One solution is to limit your exposure to the news. Find a level you can tolerate and maintain it. Another is to pray for others, those who are addicts, victims, rebels, warriors, or struck with illness. Above all, replace all your world worries with God's wisdom. Pray and memorize Bible verses to help you stay above the fray. Here's one to start you off: "You will keep in perfect peace all who trust in you, all whose thoughts are fixed on you!" (Isaiah 26:3 NLT).

Stress Less, Pray More

Understanding Prayer

I exhort therefore, that. . .supplications, prayers, intercessions, and giving of thanks, be made for all men; for kings, and for all that are in authority; that we may lead a quiet and peaceable life in all godliness and honesty. For this is good and acceptable in the sight of God.

1 Timothy 2:1–3 kjv

God wants us to live quiet and peaceful lives dedicated to Him. To help us do so, the apostle Paul lists four different kinds of prayer. *Ellicott's Commentary for English Readers* helps us understand what they are:

> The Greek word translated "supplications" signifies a request for particular benefits, and is a special form of the more general word rendered "prayers." The third expression in the English version translated "intercessions" suggests a closer and more intimate communion with God on the part of the one praying. It speaks of drawing near God, of entering into free, familiar speech with Him. The Greek word suggests prayer in its most individual, urgent form. The fourth term, "giving of thanks," expresses that which ought never to be absent from any of our devotions, gratitude for past mercies.

Praying for those in authority is our best tool for living a life of peace, even if we don't agree with those in power. F. B. Meyer writes, "It was most important that Christians should not be suspected of revolutionary designs or civic turbulence. If they had to suffer, it must be only on account of their religious faith."

For whom will you pray today?

God's Gentleness

Your gentleness has made me great.

PSALM 18:35 NKJV

We wonder sometimes when God is so great, so terrible in majesty, that He uses so little violence with us, who are so small. But it is not His way. His way is to be gentle. He seldom drives, but draws. He seldom compels, but leads. He remembers we are dust. We think it might be quicker work if God threatened and compelled us to do right. But God does not want quick work, but good work. God does not want slave work, but free work. So, God is gentle with us all—molding us and winning us many a times with no more than a silent look. Coarse treatment never wins souls. So God did not drive the chariot of His omnipotence up to Peter and command him to repent. God did not threaten him with thunderbolts of punishment. God did not even speak to him. That one look laid a spell upon his soul which was more than voice or language through all his afterlife.

God may be dealing with us in some quiet way just now and we do not know it. So mysteriously has all our life been shaped, and so unobtrusive the fingers which mold our will, that we scarce believe it has been the hand of God at all. But it is God's gentleness. And the reason why God made Peter's heart sensitive, and yours and mine, was to meet His gentleness.

HENRY DRUMMOND

Sole Recourse

O Lord, thou art my God; I will exalt thee, I will praise thy name; for thou hast done wonderful things. . . . For thou hast been a strength to the poor, a strength to the needy in his distress, a refuge from the storm, a shadow from the heat.

Isaiah 25:1, 4 kjv

When worry causes a storm of unease to rise within, your sole recourse is to turn to God. He's the only one powerful enough to calm the troubled sea of your heart. And when His peace overrides your storm, you can focus your all on Him, your Refuge.

365 Devotions on the Power of Prayer

Oh, Lord, unto whom all hearts are open, Thou canst govern the vessel of my soul far better than I can. Arise, O Lord, and command the stormy wind and the troubled sea of my heart to be still, and at peace in Thee, that I may look up to Thee undisturbed, and abide in union with Thee, my Lord. Let me not be carried hither and thither by wandering thoughts; but forgetting all else, let me see and hear Thee. Renew my spirit; kindle me in Thy light, that it may shine within me, and my heart may burn in love and adoration towards Thee. Let Thy Holy Spirit dwell in me continually, and make me Thy temple and sanctuary, and fill me with divine love and light and life, with devout and heavenly thoughts, with comfort and strength, with joy and peace. Amen.

JOHANN ARNDT

Quiet Time: Part 1

Meditate within your heart on your bed, and be still.

PSALM 4:4 NKJV

In this fast-paced, noisy world, quiet time is a precious commodity. If cell phones aren't ringing, the dog is barking or the kids are arguing. If the television isn't on, a CD player is blaring nearby. If people aren't talking, your computer is dinging, telling you that you have mail.

That's why the early morning hours are ideal for quiet time before the Lord. The morning is your chance to spend time with God before the world fully awakens. Before you rise, meditate and be still.

You may be asking, "How can I just sit here when the phone may ring?" or, "How can I rest when I have so much to do today?" There are a few easy remedies. Before you begin your quiet time with God, take the phone off the hook. Then sit in a comfortable chair or lie upon your bed. Psalm 46:10 (NIV) instructs us to "be still, and know that [He is] God." So take some time to relax each muscle and tendon. If you have trouble quieting your mind or relaxing your body, let the Lord lead you beside still waters. Think of a place that is quiet and peaceful. Imagine that place in your mind. It may be a mountaintop, beach, or forest. Now picture yourself in that scene, lying on the mountaintop, sitting on a sunny beach, or leaning against a tree trunk. Then relax and be still. Feel the peace of God.

Power Prayers to Start Your Day

Quiet Time: Part 2

He calms the storm, so that its waves are still.
PSALM 107:29 NKJV

To ready your heart and mind for a meaningful time of prayer, expect God to show up. Remember that His sole desire is to spend precious moments with you. Next, admit that God is now present, sitting in the chair beside you, ready to listen to your petitions and give you advice and direction. Finally, prepare your mind, body, and heart to receive and accept His Word and direction.

Now that your heart, mind, and body have been readied, call upon the Holy Spirit to help you pray. He will hook you up to your heavenly power source. He's ready to transform you—within and without.

So, as the Glade commercial said about the air freshener, "Plug it in, plug it in." Find your peace and then plug in to the Holy Spirit. Once you connect, the power of your prayers will be awesome, allowing you to be strengthened by the Pilot of your life as you pray for yourself, others, and the world.

God is ever ready to help us seek peace and quiet in this hectic world. So enter that quiet place, remembering that when you pray, He will listen (Jeremiah 29:12). Once you've said "Amen," don't rush off but remain silent and listen, for God is also ready to speak and to guide you through this life (Psalm 32:7). Amid His presence, you will receive His courage and strength to meet the day.

Power Prayers to Start Your Day

Your Very Breath

They should seek God, in the hope that they might feel after Him and find Him, although He is not far from each one of us. For in Him we live and move and have our being.

Acts 17:27–28 AMPC

God is not some distant, foreign object. He is closer than your very breath. Saint Gregory of Nazianus advised us to "Remember God more often than you breathe."

Imagine thinking of God with each inhale and exhale. Pause in this moment and feel that breath. Feel God's presence. Recognize He is above, below, within, and without. With these ideas at the forefront of your mind and the awareness of His love in the depths of your soul, there is no room for freeze, fright, or flight. Simply peace as you live, move, and have your being.

Pray: Lord, You are a living God working in my life, taking care of me, and bringing me peace in this very moment, as I live and breathe. Amen.

Stress Less, Pray More

Trust in the dark, trust in the light, trust at night and trust in the morning, and you will find that the faith that may begin perhaps by a mighty effort will end, sooner or later, by becoming the easy and natural habit of the soul. It is a law of spiritual life that every act of trust makes the next act less difficult, until at length, if these acts are persisted in, trusting becomes, like breathing, the natural unconscious action of the redeemed soul.

HANNAH WHITALL SMITH

Letting Go

A time to keep, and a time to cast away.

Ecclesiastes 3:6 KJV

The activity of the natural, selfish life is the greatest obstacle to your progress. Allow of nothing which gives sustenance to this life. Be on your guard against applause. Applaud not yourself when you have done well. Admit no reflections in regard to the good you have accomplished, so that all that nourishes self-complacency may die.

Possess your soul in peace as much as possible; not by effort, but by ceasing from effort; by letting go everything that troubles you. Be quiet, that you may settle, as we leave water to settle when agitated. When you discover your errors and sins, do not stop, under whatever good pretext, to remedy them. Rather abandon yourself at once to God, that he may destroy, in you, all that is displeasing to him. I assure you, you are not capable of yourself, to correct the least fault. Your only remedy is abandonment to God, and remaining quiet in his hands. If you discovered the depth of inward corruption in your heart, your courage would fail! On this account, God conceals from us, in part, the view of our sins, and discovers them to us, only as he destroys them.

Rest assured, God loves you. He will take care of you. Have faith in his love and mercy. You will see farther by and by. . . . Have good courage, and all will be well.

MADAM GUYON

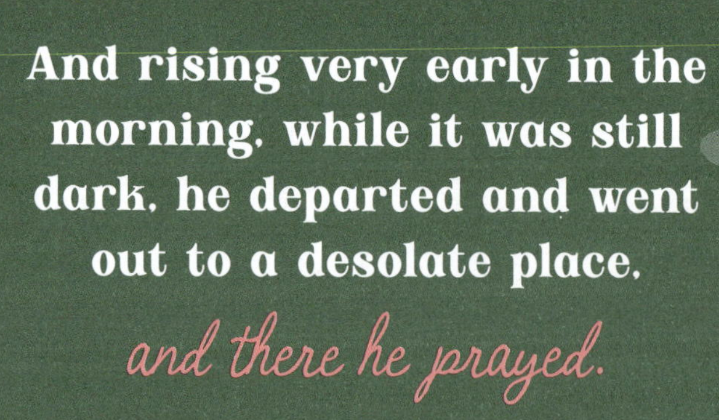
And rising very early in the morning, while it was still dark, he departed and went out to a desolate place,
and there he prayed.
Mark 1:35 ESV

Keeping the Peace

And rising very early in the morning, while it was still dark, he departed and went out to a desolate place, and there he prayed. And Simon and those who were with him searched for him, and they found him and said to him, "Everyone is looking for you."

Mark 1:35–37 ESV

Jesus worked a lot of miracles. He was up against a lot of different political and religious factions. He was pressed by the crowds that were seeking healing physically, emotionally, mentally, and spiritually. He was teaching and training disciples who just didn't seem to get it right. He was pressured by Satan who was trying to tempt Him away from His mission. He encountered people in His own hometown—even family members—who either didn't believe Him or wanted Him to tip His hand before it was time. He didn't even have a place to lay His head down. Yet in spite of all the things He was up against, Jesus never panicked but kept His peace. How? He went off alone and sought His Father God. He left the crowds and went to a deserted and desolate place. Somewhere secluded where He could meet with God one-on-one in the quiet of the morning hours.

Follow Him. On your own. Knowing the joy and peace you will feel when, in the quiet and solitude, you can speak to Him from your heart of hearts.

Stress Less, Pray More

Open Eyes

His servant said to him, "Alas, my master! What shall we do?" So he answered, "Do not fear, for those who are with us are more than those who are with them." And Elisha prayed.

2 Kings 6:15–17 NKJV

The king of Aram's attacks against Israel were not going well. Almost as soon as he told his men where he'd be battling Israel next, Elisha would whisper that location into the king of Israel's ears, preparing God's people to fend off the coming attack.

Angered, the king of Aram decided to do away with the prophet. Discovering Elisha was in Dothan, the king sent horses, chariots, and a well-armed force to capture him. They came in the darkness of night and surrounded the city.

The next morning, Elisha's servant looked out and lost his peace. He ran to Elisha, saying, "This is terrible! We have no chance against this great army!"

Elisha reassured him, saying, "Do not fear. Those with us are greater than the army without." And then he prayed, "Lord, I pray, open his eyes that he may see" (2 Kings 6:17 NKJV). The result? "The Lord opened the servant's eyes, and he saw; and behold, the mountain was full of horses and chariots of fire all around Elisha" (2 Kings 6:17 NASB).

When the enemy army attacked, Elisha prayed again, asking God to strike the men with blindness. And God answered his prayer.

When things look hopeless and you lose your peace, pray. Then open your eyes to God's reality as He restores your peace.

Underlying Peace

Fear not: . . .thou art mine.

Isaiah 43:1 KJV

Your vision of the world affects your world—both inner and outer. Pray for yourself and others to have a godly and peace-filled perspective. It will change the world.

O Thou, who art the ever-blessed God, the underlying Peace of the world, and who wouldst draw all men into the companionship of Thy joy; speak, we beseech Thee, to this Thy servant, for whom we pray. Take him by the hand and say unto him, "Fear not; for I am with thee. I have called thee by my name; thou art mine." Put such a spirit of trust within him that all fear and foreboding shall be cast out, and that right reason and calm assurance may rule his thoughts and impulses. Let quietness and confidence be his strength. Reveal to him the vision of a universe guided and governed by Thy wise and loving care; and show him that around and about him are Thy unseen and beneficent powers. Lift up his whole being into communion with Thy life and thought. Let him ever remember that Thou dost not give to any the spirit of fearfulness, but a spirit of power and love and self-mastery. In this faith, grant, O Lord, that he may summon the energies of his soul against the miseries that cast him down. Give him courage, confidence, an untroubled heart, and a love that loves all creatures, great and small, for Thy love's sake. Amen.

Samuel McComb

The Most Powerful Form of Energy

Paul and Silas were praying and singing hymns to God. . . . Suddenly, there was a massive earthquake, and the prison was shaken to its foundations. All the doors immediately flew open, and the chains of every prisoner fell off!

Acts 16:25–26 NLT

"Prayer is not only worship; it is also an invisible emanation of man's worshiping spirit—the most powerful form of energy that one can generate," wrote Nobel prizewinner Alexis Carrel, MD.

Prayer is a force that can shake open doors, make chains fall away, and set prisoners free. With all this power, it's obvious prayer can release your stress, make your burdens fall away, and change your limited perspective. All you need to do is believe it is possible. When you do, you will be singing with the chorus, "Our Lord is great, with limitless strength" (Psalm 147:5 MSG).

Today pray: "I want to tap into Your power, Lord. I know there is nothing too hard or impossible for You. Help me generate the prayer power to let You in and break my chains. To give me the peace I seek and the calm I crave. In Jesus' name I pray, amen."

Stress Less, Pray More

Those persons who know the deep peace of God, the unfathomable peace that passeth all understanding, are always men and women of much prayer.

R. A. TORREY

The Bare God

He only is my rock and my salvation:
he is my defence; I shall not be moved.
PSALM 62:6 KJV

No soul can be really at rest until it has given up all dependence on everything else and has been forced to depend on the Lord alone. Feelings may change, and will change, with our changing circumstances; prayers may seem to lose their fervency; promises may seem to fail; everything that we have believed in or depended upon may seem to be swept away, and only God is left, just God, the bare God, if I may be allowed that expression; simply and only God.

Promises may be misunderstood or misplaced or misapplied, and, at the moment when we are leaning all our weight upon them, they may seem utterly to fail us. But the Promiser, who stands behind His promises and is infinitely more than His promises, can never fail nor change. The little child does not need to have promises from his mother to make him content; it has its mother himself, and she is enough. Mother is better than a thousand promises. In our highest ideal of love or friendship, promises do not enter. The personality of lover or friend is better than all their promises. If every promise should be wiped out of the Bible, we would still have God left, and God would be enough. Again I repeat it, only God, He Himself, just as He is, without addition of anything on our part.

HANNAH WHITALL SMITH

Patience, Comfort, and Hope

Whatever things were written before were written for our learning, that we through the patience and comfort of the Scriptures might have hope. . . . "As for Me," says the LORD, "this is My covenant with them: My Spirit who is upon you, and My words which I have put in your mouth, shall not depart from your mouth, nor from the mouth of your descendants, nor from the mouth of your descendants' descendants," says the LORD, "from this time and forevermore."

ROMANS 15:4; ISAIAH 59:21 NKJV

How much important matter do we find condensed in this single verse [Romans 15:4]! What a light and glory does it throw on the Word of God! It has been well noted that we have here *its authority*; as it is a written word; *its antiquity*, as it was written aforetime; *its utility*, as it is written for our learning. We may also infer from what immediately follows, *its divine origin*; for, if by means of the holy scriptures, and the power of the Holy Spirit (Isaiah 59:21), God imparts to our soul patience and comfort and hope, because He is the God of patience and comfort and hope. He is the fountain of these gifts and graces, which by the channel of His inspired Word, flow into our hearts and lives, to strengthen us for service.

S. D. GORDON

When They Were Quiet

Did not our heart burn within us, while he talked with us by the way, and while he opened to us the scriptures?

Luke 24:32 KJV

Look back to the road that leads to Emmaus, and to two men, one named Cleopas, the other a nameless disciple. Listen to them, on this day after the Crucifixion, speaking among themselves. They had lost their hope, and they had lost their confidence in Jesus' ability to do what they thought He was going to do. Their attitude toward Jesus was the attitude of men who should say, "Oh, we believe in Him, we love Him. He meant well, but He has not succeeded. We had *hoped* that it was He who should redeem Israel." Their hope was gone. . . .

This is the picture of these men as they set their faces toward Emmaus. [Until a Stranger joins them on the road and engages them in conversations concerning the events in Jerusalem. When at last the Stranger sits with the men for a meal, they recognize Him as Jesus.]

How did Christ deal with these hopeless men? I freely confess I am surprised at the wonder of His coming to these men. Why does He come? He comes because He is seeking love. It was there in those doubt-shadowed hearts, and He knew it. What were the things He said to them? Nothing new. He opened the scriptures to them. When they were quiet, they heard Him speak to them. Then their hearts burned with hope.

G. CAMPBELL MORGAN

Still Waters

He leadeth me beside the still waters.

Psalm 23:2 KJV

A man may believe forever that his sins will be forgiven at some future time, and he will never find peace. He has to come to the *now* belief and say by a present appropriating faith, "My sins are now forgiven," before his soul can be at rest. And similarly, no faith that looks for a future deliverance from the power of sin will ever lead a soul into the life we are describing. . . .

Perhaps no four words in the language have more meaning in them than the following, which I would have you repeat over and over with your voice and with your soul, emphasizing each time a different word:

Jesus saves me now—It is He.

Jesus *saves* me now—It is His work to save.

Jesus saves *me* now—I am the one to be saved.

Jesus saves me *now*—He is doing it every moment. . . .

In order to enter into this blessed interior life of rest and triumph, you have two steps to take—first, entire abandonment; and second, absolute faith. No matter what may be the complications of your peculiar experience, no matter what your difficulties or your surroundings or your "peculiar temperament," these two steps, definitely taken and unwaveringly persevered in, will certainly bring you out sooner or later into the green pastures and still waters of this life hid with Christ in God.

HANNAH WHITALL SMITH, *The Christian's Secret of a Happy Life*

Will Do as Promised

May the God of peace set you apart for Himself. May every part of you be set apart for God. May your spirit and your soul and your body be kept complete. . . . The One Who called you is faithful and will do what He promised.

1 Thessalonians 5:23–24 NLV

There is nothing more comforting in this world than the promises of God. Yet the promises themselves are not enough. What is needed is to apply faith in those promises. To have the firm conviction that God will do what He said, that He will keep His word.

Why? Because He loves us. And because He cannot lie. Numbers 23:19 (AMPC) says, "God is not a man, that He should tell or act a lie, neither the son of man, that He should feel repentance or compunction [for what He has promised]. Has He said and shall He not do it? Or has He spoken and shall He not make it good?"

Even though the promises of God may sound not just extraordinary but unrealistic, especially to a nonbeliever, put all your faith in them. For God does the impossible over and over again, both for you and everyone else who is familiar with Him. And His promises are gifts that you don't return but rely on.

The highest pinnacle of the spiritual life is not happy joy in unbroken sunshine, but absolute and undoubting trust in the love of God.

A. W. THOROLD

Praise for Peace: Part 1

Give thanks to him and praise his name.

PSALM 100:4 NLT

What a privilege to approach God, to bow down before Him, laud Him with our praises, and feel His presence within us! Sometimes, as we draw near, appropriate words evade us. Yet all is not lost, for God has given us a powerful, praise-filled resource—the book of Psalms.

In the midst of praising our Lord and Savior, our lives are transformed in several ways. First and foremost, our spirits become intimately connected with His. As we lift our voices, extolling His name and deeds, we are invaded by His presence. "But You are holy, O You Who dwell in [the holy place where]. . .praises. . .[are offered]" (Psalm 22:3 AMPC). God abides within us when we praise Him!

Second, when we praise God our fears are allayed. Psalm 56:10–11 (NIV) says, "In God, whose word I praise, in the LORD, whose word I praise—in God I trust and am not afraid." There is no room for fear where praise has taken up residence.

Third, praise changes our outlook as we view our world through the eyes of our Creator (Psalm 103:1, 5). Suddenly, when we see things from the perspective of the One who made and sustains the entire universe, the cares of this world grow dim.

Power Prayers to Start Your Day

Praise for Peace: Part 2

"We do not know what to do, but our eyes are on you."
2 Chronicles 20:12 NIV

Fourth, praise vanquishes our enemy. Second Chronicles 20 tells the story of when Jehoshaphat, king of Judah, was faced with a vast army coming against him. He prayed the verses above to the Lord. The people bowed down and worshipped Him. The next morning, Jehoshaphat appointed his men to sing to the Lord and praise His name. They went out into the front lines, ahead of the army, saying, "Give thanks to the Lord, for his love endures forever" (v. 21 NIV). The result? Not only was that day's foe vanquished (the enemy armies ended up destroying each other), but for the remainder of Jehoshaphat's reign, "God [gave] him rest on every side" (v. 30 NIV).

And finally, our love for God is deepened when we adore Him and give Him thanks for past blessings. It is then we are reminded of the great love of the Father (Psalm 103:11).

After the sun rises but before you approach God with your daily petitions, get into the praise mode, reminding Him (and yourself) how terrific He is, how awed you are to have Him in your life, how blessed you are that He came down to earth to save *you*. Drench yourself in the words of praise of the Psalms. Sing a familiar worship song! Have no reservations as you come into His presence. And as you speak to your Creator, through His Word, He will speak to you.

Power Prayers to Start Your Day

Faith in the Power of Prayer

The first thing I want you to do is pray. Pray every way you know how, for everyone you know. Pray especially for rulers and their governments to rule well so we can be quietly about our business of living simply, in humble contemplation. This is the way our Savior God wants us to live.

1 TIMOTHY 2:1–3 MSG

The great thing about prayer is that it not only changes and affects our world, but it changes and affects ourselves.

So, if you're tired of the status quo, if you want to change things for the better in the world within and without, take up the power of prayer every day. Believe that it will change things, that your petitions are rising up like incense to the throne of God. Encourage others to do the same. Then watch God work, inside and out.

What a faith in the power of prayer! A few feeble and despised Christians are to influence the mighty Roman emperors and help in securing peace and quietness. Let us believe that prayer is a power that is taken up by God in His rule of the world. Let us pray for our country and its rulers; for all the rulers of the world; for rulers in cities or districts in which we are interested. When God's people unite in this, they may count upon their prayer effecting in the unseen world more than they know. Let faith hold this fast.

ANDREW MURRAY

Carried

Listen to Me [says the Lord], . . .you who have been borne by Me from your birth, carried from the womb: Even to your old age I am He, and even to hair white with age will I carry you. I have made, and I will bear; yes, I will carry and will save you.

Isaiah 46:3–4 AMPC

There's something disconcerting about realizing you're getting old. One woman, upon seeing her first gray hair, thought it had somehow fallen on her head from the ceiling. But when she reached up to remove it from her head, the pain from her plucking told her otherwise.

Aging begins to happen as soon as we're born. When we are young, we brag about our age. When we are old, we work on ignoring it. Either way, young or old, we can find peace that God will continue to be with us. After all, He is the One that formed us. He carried us as newborns and will continue to do so when we're old and gray. So keep your peace. God's got this. God's got you.

O Father, thou art my eternity.
Not on the clasp of consciousness—on thee
My life depends; and I can well afford
All to forget, so thou remember, Lord.
In thee I rest; in sleep thou dost me fold;
In thee I labour; still in thee, grow old;
And dying, shall I not in thee, my Life, be bold?

George MacDonald

Faith rests on the naked
Word of God.
When we take Him
at His Word,
the heart is at peace.

At His Word

I will listen [with expectancy] to what God the Lord will say, for He will speak peace to His people, to His saints (those who are in right standing with Him)—but let them not turn again to [self-confident] folly.

Psalm 85:8 AMPC

Today, put your ear up to God's lips. Listen, expecting He will speak to you. Know that His words will bring the balm of calm to your soul. That His words you can trust.

When we believe that God hears us, it is but natural that we should be eager to hear him. Only from him can come the word which can speak peace to troubled spirits; the voices of men are feeble in such a case. . . ; but God's voice is power, he speaks and it is done, and hence when we hear him our distress is ended. Happy is the suppliant who has grace to lie patiently at the Lord's door, and wait until his love shall act according to its old wont and chase all sorrow far away. "For he will speak peace unto his people, and to his saints."

CHARLES SPURGEON, *The Treasury of David*

Faith has nothing to do with feelings or with impressions, with improbabilities or with outward experiences. If we desire to couple such things with faith, then we are no longer resting on the Word of God, because faith needs nothing of the kind. Faith rests on the naked Word of God. When we take Him at His Word, the heart is at peace.

GEORGE MUELLER

Calm as a Baby

Light, space, zest—that's GOD! So, with him on my side I'm fearless, afraid of no one and nothing. . . . When besieged, I'm calm as a baby. When all hell breaks loose, I'm collected and cool. I'm asking GOD for one thing, only one thing: To live with him in his house my whole life long. I'll contemplate his beauty; I'll study at his feet.

PSALM 27:1, 3–4 MSG

All the "what if" supposing in life can leave a sister bereft of peace. For that worrywart's focus is no longer on the Word and frame of one called Jesus Christ but is on the myriad of possibilities that may never come to pass. What a waste of God-given energy for the distracted diva whose song of trust, triumph, and tranquility is being drowned out by worldly woes.

Better that she was concerned about only one thing—dwelling in God's Word, beholding His beauty, and meditating in His temple. For in His presence, no evil, no worry, no "what ifs" can reach her. He is a strong tower, a refuge, a depository for her cares.

It is a wise woman who accepts Jesus Christ as the taker of her cares. She knows that when she commits herself—mind, body, spirit, soul, and heart—and her life to the Lord, she is in the best of places, reposing at His feet, listening to His voice, praising His name, and simply resting, trusting He will see her through every situation.

Sweet Hour of Prayer

Heaven in Mind

Be of good courage, and he shall strengthen your heart, all ye that hope in the Lord. . . .Let not your heart be troubled, neither let it be afraid.

Psalm 31:24; John 14:27 KJV

One evening when Luther saw a little bird perched on a tree, to roost there for the night, he said, "This little bird has had its supper, and now it is getting ready to go to sleep here, quite secure and content, never troubling itself what its food will be, or where its lodging on the morrow. Like David, it 'abides under the shadow of the Almighty' [Psalm 91:1]. It sits on its little twig content, and lets God take care."

MARTIN LUTHER

A true Christian, that hath power over his own will, may live nobly and happily, and enjoy a clear heaven within the serenity of his own mind perpetually. When the sea of this world is most rough and tempestuous about him, then can he ride safely at anchor within the haven, by a sweet compliance of his will with God's will. He can look about him, and with an even and indifferent mind behold the world either to smile or frown upon him; neither will he abate of the least of his contentment for all the ill and unkind usage he meets withal in this life. He that hath got the mastery over his own will feels no violence from without, finds no contests.

JOHN SMITH

Rise Up in Peace

Humble yourselves therefore under the mighty hand of God, that he may exalt you in due time: Casting all your care upon him; for he careth for you.

1 Peter 5:6–7 KJV

Worry is like a dark, heavy cloud of distorted thoughts that comes between you and the Prince of Peace. It follows you around, keeping you from seeing the light Christ would shine upon your mind. It's formed when you're in a place of uncertainty, when you panic, thinking you have to come up with your own solutions. But your God is a God of certainty and wisdom. So put all your what-ifs in His hands. And thank Him for all the what-ares in your life. When you do, He'll remove from you all the faithless fears that weigh you down and may never come to pass. Pray for Christ to beam His light upon you. Then rise up in peace and victory.

365 Devotions on the Power of Prayer

O most loving Father, you who will us to give thanks for all things, to dread nothing but the loss of yourself, and to cast all our care on you, who care for us; preserve us from faithless fears and worldly anxieties, and grant that no clouds of this mortal life may hide from us the light of that love which is immortal, and which you have manifested unto us in your Son, Jesus Christ our Lord.

WILLIAM BRIGHT

Afterward

Afterward it yieldeth the peaceable fruit.

Hebrews 12:11 KJV

How happy are tried Christians afterward. There is no calm more deep than that which succeeds a storm. Who has not rejoiced in clear skies after rain? Our sorrows, like the passing keels of the vessels upon the sea, leave a silver line of holy light behind them "afterward." It is peace—sweet, deep peace—which follows the horrible turmoil which once reigned in our tormented, guilty souls.

The Christian has his best things last, and he therefore in this world receives his worst things first. But even his worst things are "afterward" good things. Even now he grows rich by his losses, he rises by his falls, he lives by dying and becomes full by being emptied; if then his grievous afflictions yield him so much peaceable fruit in this life, what shall be the full vintage of joy "afterward" in heaven?

If his dark nights are as bright as the world's days, what shall his days be? If even his starlight is more splendid than the sun, what must his sunlight be? If he can sing in a dungeon, how sweetly will he sing in heaven? If he can praise the Lord in the fires, how will he extol Him before the eternal throne? If evil be good to him now, what will the overflowing goodness of God be to him then?

Who would not choose to be a Christian? Who would not bear the present cross for the crown which cometh afterward? Wait, dear soul, and let patience have her perfect work.

CHARLES SPURGEON

A Covenant of Peace

"For the mountains shall depart and the hills be removed, but My kindness shall not depart from you, nor shall My covenant of peace be removed," says the LORD, who has mercy on you.

ISAIAH 54:10 NKJV

Looking forward to future dangers, and in defiance of them, God's favors appear constant and His kindness everlasting, for it is formed into a covenant of peace.

This is as firm as the waters of Noah, that is, as firm as that promise God made concerning the deluge, that there should never be the like again (Genesis 8:21–22; 9:11). God has kept His word, though the world has been very provoking. And thus inviolable is the covenant of grace: "I have sworn that I would not be angry with you, as I have been, nor rebuke you, as I have done" (Isaiah 54:9).

It is more firm than the strongest parts of the visible creation. "The mountains shall depart and the hills be removed." Mountains have sometimes been shaken by earthquakes and removed, but the promises of God were never broken by the shock of any event. When our friends fail us, our God does not, nor does His kindness depart. Do the kings of the earth and the rulers set themselves against the Lord? They shall depart and be removed. God's kindness shall never depart from His people, for whomever He loves, He loves to the end. Therefore, the covenant is immovable and inviolable, because it is built not on our merit but on God's mercy.

MATTHEW HENRY

Under God's Wings

Be merciful and gracious to me, O God, be merciful and gracious to me, for my soul takes refuge and finds shelter and confidence in You; yes, in the shadow of Your wings will I take refuge and be confident until calamities and destructive storms are passed.

Psalm 57:1 AMPC

When nothing in your life seems to be going right, when your heart won't stop racing, when a good night's sleep is a distant dream, when you're panicking, when you can't catch your breath, stop. Breathe deep. And allow yourself to be led to the refuge found under the shadow of God's wings (Psalm 57:1; 63:7; 91:4).

There, in that place of peace and quiet, things are right. There, you are protected from the world. There, you can find the sleep that you need. There, you can trust you will be safe. There, you can catch your breath, close your eyes, and calm your heart. There, you can wait until the calamities and storms have passed by.

Jesus once offered this place of refuge to God's people—in fact He was dying to do so—but found no takers (Matthew 23:37). So He died to allow them and us to come to our senses, to come to Him and shelter beneath His wings of peace.

Be wise, be willing, beneath the wings of Christ. And you will find all the calm and space you need for true peace.

No Fear: Part 1

And they who know Your name [who have experience and acquaintance with Your mercy] will lean on and confidently put their trust in You, for You, Lord, have not forsaken those who seek (inquire of and for) You.

Psalm 9:10 AMPC

Fear comes in many sizes, shapes, and forms. There's a writer's fear of facing a blank page, a mother's fear of harm coming to her child, a father's fear of losing his job, a grandparent's fear of death, a banker's fear of being robbed, a soldier's fear of being killed, a country's fear of terrorist attacks—within and without.

When fear invades our spirits, we need to turn to the One in whom we have confidence—Jesus Christ, the Good Shepherd. The One who tells us that He is with us always, "to the very end of the age" (Matthew 28:20 NIV).

Although we may not understand why certain things happen in our lives, God instructs us to be strong and courageous, for "no one will be able to stand against you all the days of your life. . . . I will be with you; I will never leave you nor forsake you" (Joshua 1:5 NIV). Do you have this confidence—that God is with you in the storms of life? That you can trust in Him and He will bring you through it all? Or do you trust in something other than Christ? "Some trust in chariots and some in horses, but we trust in the name of the Lord our God" (Psalm 20:7 NIV).

Power Prayers to Start Your Day

No Fear: Part 2

I will fear no evil, for you are with me.

Psalm 23:4 NIV

The only confidence we have in this life is knowing God is always with us. He's our protector, comforter, and guide. And if we are wise enough, we will look for and find God in every moment, filled with the assurance that He is with us through the good and the bad, the known and the unknown, the beginning and the end. He is there when others are not. If we follow God—through prayer and the reading and application of His Word—He will keep us close to Him, traveling down the right path, until we reach our home, where He greets us. Within the shelter of His embrace, fear is vanquished.

Be a person with powerful confidence in Christ. Renew your mind each and every morning with God's truth, for that truth is what will keep you confident and expectant throughout the day. Plant God's Word in your heart and mind. Pray for His deliverance: "Deliver me from evil." Leave your fears at His feet.

Reflect on your past experiences, how God has carried you through. Go to your protector, guide, and Good Shepherd, for He and His Word are the only things that can set you free from all fear as you trust and hope in Him. Know that "[God] will order his angels to protect you wherever you go. They will hold you up with their hands so you won't even hurt your foot on a stone" (Psalm 91:11–12 NLT).

Power Prayers to Start Your Day

True Prayer

"Here's what I want you to do: Find a quiet, secluded place so you won't be tempted to role-play before God. Just be there as simply and honestly as you can manage. The focus will shift from you to God, and you will begin to sense his grace."

MATTHEW 6:6 MSG

A true prayer is an inventory of wants, a catalogue of necessities, a revelation of hidden poverty. While it is an application to divine wealth, it is a confession of human emptiness.

The most healthy state of a Christian is to be always empty in self and constantly depending upon the Lord for supplies, to be always poor in self and rich in Jesus. Prayer is in itself, apart from the answer that it brings, a great benefit to the Christian. As the runner gains strength for the race by daily exercise, so for the great race of life, we acquire energy by the hallowed labor of prayer. An earnest pleader comes out of his closet, even as the sun rises from the chambers of the east, rejoicing like a strong man to run his race.

Prayer girds human weakness with divine strength, turns human folly into heavenly wisdom, and gives to troubled mortals the peace of God. We know not what prayer cannot do! We thank You, great God, for the mercy seat, a choice proof of Your marvelous loving-kindness. Help us to use it in the right manner throughout this day!

CHARLES SPURGEON

Believe and Wait

I would have lost heart, unless I had believed that I would see the goodness of the LORD in the land of the living. Wait on the LORD; be of good courage, and He shall strengthen your heart; wait, I say, on the LORD!

PSALM 27:13–14 NKJV

What does a woman do when all seems lost? When she's ready to give herself up to darkness and despair because there seems to be no hope, no hope at all? She digs deep within herself and draws upon her faith.

Over and over again God shows you how He can do the impossible when you find yourself stranded between an army of problems and a sea of despair. Just when you think there's no way out, God in His goodness parts the waters, giving you hope that you will live to see another day. All you had to do was trust in Him and wait.

Today, believe that you will see God's goodness enter into your situation. All you need to do is stay calm and have courage. God will give you the strength to do so.

My prayers, my God, flow from what I am not;
I think thy answers make me what I am.
Like weary waves thought follows upon thought,
But the still depth beneath is all thine own,
And there thou mov'st in paths to us unknown.
Out of strange strife thy peace is strangely wrought;
If the lion in us pray—thou answerest the lamb.

GEORGE MACDONALD

Our Avenue

"Let not your hearts be troubled. Believe in God; believe also in me." . . . "Peace I leave with you; my peace I give to you. Not as the world gives do I give to you. Let not your hearts be troubled, neither let them be afraid."

JOHN 14:1, 27 ESV

Stress is nothing to be ashamed of. It's just a signal to be recognized and addressed. The problems arise when we let it take over, try to ignore it, or imagine we can handle it in our own strength.

God knew we'd have trouble in this life, that we'd find ourselves with anxiety-causing stress. But He also gave us a way out: Jesus. Our faith in Him is our avenue to an out-of-this-world peace.

Jesus is waiting. Take a deep belly breath. Exhale. Enter that secret place where He abides. Ask Him to cover you with His wings, to raise you up. To give you the Word you need to hear, the peace you need to inhale. Try praying a prayer, saying something like, "I'm here, Lord, limp in Your arms. Fill me with Your peace." Make sure it comes from your heart. And He'll answer.

Stress Less, Pray More

Ye do well to remember that habitual affectionate communion with God, asking Him for all good which is needed, praising Him for all that is received, and trusting Him for future supplies, prevents anxious cares, inspires peace, calmness and composure, and furnishes a delight surpassing all finite comprehension.

JAMES H. AUGHEY

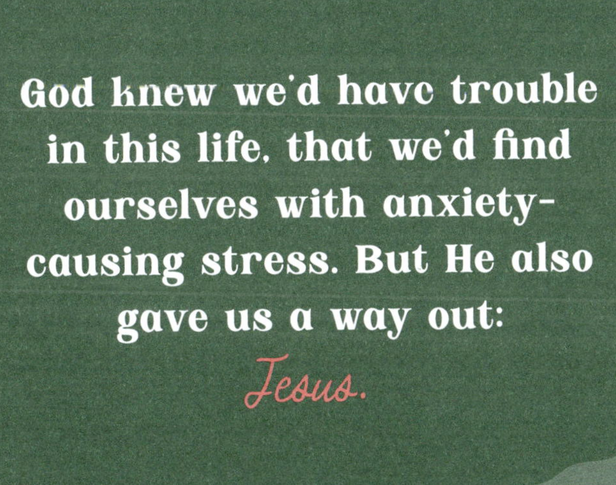
God knew we'd have trouble
in this life, that we'd find
ourselves with anxiety-
causing stress. But He also
gave us a way out:
Jesus.

Taking Care

"He felt compassion for him. . . . [The Samaritan] took care of him. The next day he handed the innkeeper two silver coins, telling him, 'Take care of this man.'"

LUKE 10:33–35 NLT

A man had been stripped and beaten by robbers. Afterward, a priest went by. Seeing the man lying there, the priest continued on his way. Then a religious man did the same. Finally, a Samaritan (a race hated by the Jews) came along. He saw the man and was moved with compassion. He dressed the man's wounds, put him on his donkey, and took him to an inn. There he continued to take care of him. The next day, he gave the innkeeper money to do the same until he got back.

Jesus is *our* Good Samaritan, the One who takes care of us. Hated by His Jewish brothers and sisters, He stops, has compassion on us, and tends our wounds.

What peace we find when we—robbed of joy, beaten and bruised by forces inside and out, wanting and needing our wounds healed—are met with compassion by Jesus. May we go and do the same.

Notice those two clauses, *He took care of him* and *Take care of him*. It is thus that our Lord deals with us. When we are too far gone to ask for His help, He comes to our side and restores our ebbing life; and He raises up others to do the same.

F. B. MEYER, *Bible Commentary*

Soul Sanctuary

The Lord is my rock, and my fortress, and my deliverer; the God of my rock; in him will I trust; he is my shield, and the horn of my salvation, my high tower, and my refuge, my saviour; thou savest me from violence.

2 Samuel 22:2–3 KJV

We see that our dwelling place is also our fortress and our high tower and our rock and our refuge. We all know what a fortress is. It is a place of safety, where everything that is weak and helpless can be hidden from the enemy and kept in security. And when we are told that God, who is our dwelling place, is also our fortress, it can only mean one thing, and that is, if we will but live in our dwelling place, we shall be perfectly safe and secure from every assault of every possible enemy that can attack. "For in the time of trouble he shall hide me in his pavilion: in the secret of his tabernacle shall he hide me; he shall set me up upon a rock" (Psalm 27:5 KJV). "He that dwelleth in the secret place of the most High shall abide under the shadow of the Almighty" (Psalm 91:1 KJV). He shall hide us in the secret of His presence from the pride of man; He shall keep us secretly in a pavilion from the strife of tongues.

Trials may come in abundance, but they cannot penetrate into the sanctuary of the soul, and we may dwell in perfect peace even in the midst of life's fiercest storms.

HANNAH WHITALL SMITH

Breathe Deep

When the doors were shut where the disciples were assembled for fear of the Jews, [Jesus came] and stood in the midst, and saith unto them, Peace be unto you. And when he had so said, he shewed unto them his hands and his side. Then were the disciples glad, when they saw the Lord. Then said Jesus to them again, Peace be unto you: as my Father hath sent me, even so send I you. And when he had said this, he breathed on them, and saith unto them, Receive ye the Holy Ghost.

JOHN 20:19–22 KJV

Jesus has come to stand in your midst. His first words are "Peace be unto you." He shows you His hands and side, the wounds He suffered to save you, to bring you into the fold. Your heart rejoices, for you feel His light, power, joy, and love. He says, again, "Peace be unto you," and now you really feel it.

And then the Holy Three come into play. Jesus says, "As my Father hath sent me, even so send I you" (John 20:21 KJV). You feel His breath upon you as you hear His words, "Receive ye the Holy Ghost" (v. 22 KJV). Breathe. Breathe in Jesus' presence, God's love, and the Holy Spirit's power. Today, ask God to teach you how to breathe deeply in faith.

365 Devotions on the Power of Prayer

O God. . .teach me to breathe deeply in faith.

SØREN KIERKEGAARD

A Benediction of Peace

Peace I leave with you, my peace I give unto you.
JOHN 14:27 KJV

Beloved friends, as you go to your families, as you go through life, as you go into eternity, I pray that you "go in peace." It is heaven here on earth to possess "the peace of God which passeth all understanding." Peace should be the continual portion of all believers.

This is what the angels sang when our Lord Jesus appeared on earth: "Glory to God in the highest, and on earth peace, goodwill toward men." And as it was at the beginning of our Savior's life, it was also at the end, for this was our Lord's legacy to all His disciples: "Peace I leave with you, my peace I give unto you." He who is called "the God of peace" should be very precious to your soul.

Peace is the result of what the Savior has done for you. Has He forgiven you? Then you have peace. Has He saved you? Then feel an inward peace that no one can take from you! Did He die for you? Then you can never die in the full meaning of the word. Has He risen for you? Then because He lives, you will live, also; so do not let your heart be troubled, but be at peace. Will He come again to receive you to Himself? Then let your peace be like a river flowing from the very throne of God!

CHARLES SPURGEON

An Answer of Peace

As for me, I will call upon God, and the LORD shall save me. Evening and morning and at noon I will pray, and cry aloud, and He shall hear my voice.

PSALM 55:16–17 NKJV

When was the last time you truly sought out God? When have you called upon Him with real passion in your heart and confidence in your words?

Today, set yourself apart from the crowd, knowing you are in the right place: before God, waiting on Him, seeking an answer of peace to your prayers.

David persevered in his resolution to call upon God, being well assured that he should not seek Him in vain. "As for me, let them take what course they please to secure themselves, let violence and strife be their guards, prayer shall be mine; this I have found comfort in, and therefore this will I abide by: I will call upon God, and commit myself to Him, and the Lord shall save me. I will pray and cry aloud. I will meditate."

He will pray frequently, every day, and three times a day—evening, morning, and at noon. Those who think three meals a day little enough for the body ought much more to think three solemn prayers a day little enough for the soul and to count it a pleasure, not a task. It was Daniel's practice to pray three times a day, and noon was one of Peter's hours of prayer. David assured himself that God would in due time give an answer of peace to his prayers.

ANDREW MURRAY

Heavenly Confidence, Peace, and Strength

Wherefore seeing we also are compassed about with so great a cloud of witnesses, let us lay aside every weight, and the sin which doth so easily beset us, and let us run with patience the race that is set before us.

Hebrews 12:1 KJV

Are there days when you feel all alone in your troubles and challenges? If so, remember those who have gone before. Women who have done amazing things, blazed the trail for others, stood up for their faith, their God. Women who have overcome. Allow the thought of those who have walked the earth before you to comfort and inspire you, to give you the heavenly confidence, peace, and strength to do and endure, against all odds.

We are compassed about by a cloud of witnesses, whose hearts throb in sympathy with every effort and struggle, and who thrill with joy at every success. How should this thought check and rebuke every worldly feeling and unworthy purpose, and enshrine us, in the midst of a forgetful and unspiritual world, with an atmosphere of heavenly peace! They have overcome—have risen—are crowned, glorified; but still they remain to us, our assistants, our comforters, and in every hour of darkness their voice speaks to us: "So we grieved, so we struggled, so we fainted, so we doubted; but we have overcome, we have obtained, we have seen, we have found—and in our victory behold the certainty of thy own."

HARRIET BEECHER STOWE

The Value of Christ's Peace

"Peace I leave with you, My peace I give to you; not as the world gives do I give to you. Let not your heart be troubled, neither let it be afraid."

JOHN 14:27 NKJV

When Christ was about to leave the world, He made His will. What should He leave to His poor disciples who had left all for Him? Silver and gold He had not, but He left them what was infinitely better—His peace. He did not part in anger but in love, for this was His farewell, "Peace I leave with you."

The legacy that is here bequeathed was peace. Peace is put for all good. Peace is put for reconciliation and love. The peace bequeathed is peace with God. Peace in our own hearts seems to be specially meant. It is the peace on which the angels congratulated men at His birth (Luke 2:14).

This legacy is left to His disciples and followers. This legacy was left to them and their successors, to them and all true Christians in all ages. It is left not as the world gives. It is not a mere formality, but a real blessing. The world's gifts concern only the body and time; Christ's gifts enrich the soul for eternity. The peace Christ gives is infinitely more valuable than that which the world gives. . . .

What use should they make of this gift? "Let not your heart be troubled, neither let it be afraid."

MATTHEW HENRY

A New Way

Thus says the Lord, Who makes a way through the sea and a path through the mighty waters, . . . Do not [earnestly] remember the former things; neither consider the things of old. Behold, I am doing a new thing! Now it springs forth; do you not perceive and know it and will you not give heed to it? I will even make a way in the wilderness and rivers in the desert.

Isaiah 43:16, 18–19 AMPC

You have chosen to walk a new road. To trust the One who makes a way where you can see no way, the One who has forgiven and forgotten all the mistakes you've made.

So put your hand in the hand of the One who is ready to do a new thing in your life. Forget what has passed. Look to God in confidence, knowing He has already cleared a path for you, the precious daughter He has called by name (see Isaiah 43:1). Answer His call and walk forward in His presence.

Stress Less, Pray More

At the beginning of each new day, we must yield ourselves to His holy presence. It means a voluntary, intentional, and wholehearted turning away from the world to wait on God to make Himself known to our souls. It means making time to allow Him to reveal Himself. It is impossible to expect the abiding presence of Christ with us through the day without the daily exercise of strong desire and childlike trust in His word.

Andrew Murray

Circle of Protection

God's angel sets up a circle of protection around us while we pray. Open your mouth and taste, open your eyes and see—how good God is. Blessed are you who run to him. Worship God if you want the best; worship opens doors to all his goodness.

Psalm 34:7–9 msg

Amid a stressful situation where you see no way out—mentally, physically, emotionally, spiritually—go to God. And as soon as you're in His presence, He'll set up, between you and whatever's coming against you, a protective barrier. See it. Know it's there. Do not doubt. Then open your mouth and pray. Realize how good God is. Praise Him for what He's doing in your life. Know that even if you still don't see a way out, that's okay. You're with the Master Planner and Protector. He's got you covered. He's got an exit plan. He's got good things lined up and coming your way. Then rest in His peace.

Stress Less, Pray More

God makes use of the attendance of good spirits, for the protection of his people from the malice and power of evil spirits, and more good offices the holy angels do us daily than we are aware of. Though. . .they have constant employment in the upper world. . .yet, in obedience to their Maker, and in love to those that bear his image, they condescend to minister to the saints, and stand up for them. . . . They not only visit them, but encamp round about them, acting for their good.

Joseph Benson Commentary

Unmoved

God is in the midst of her; she shall not be moved;
God will help her when morning dawns.
Psalm 46:5 esv

No matter what troubles you're facing or what worries are on your mind, you have a mighty fortress in God. He's your "refuge and strength, an ever-present help in times of trouble" (Psalm 46:1 gw). Because He is living within you and you're abiding in Him, you cannot be harmed or moved. He brings His full power, all His angels, all His resources, visible and invisible, material and temporal, to aid you. He shields, empowers, and frees you. God brings His peace to you, telling you, gently, "I've got this. You need not worry." He tells you your role in all this. It's to simply "let be and be still, and know (recognize and understand) that I am God" (Psalm 46:10 ampc). Today, make it your aim to let be and be still. Know your God is taking care of everything. He's got this.

Worry Less, Pray More

Peace must fill your hearts and lives, and then you will find that ills and difficulties and sorrows and changes leave you unmoved. Practice that steadfast immobility, no matter what may threaten. This spirit of calm trust is the shield that turns aside the darts and stings of adversity. Practice it. Then you must seek to abide at the heart of the Universe with [God], at the center with [Him]. There alone is changelessness and calm.

God Calling at Eventide

True Hope

Oh! May the God of green hope fill you up with joy, fill you up with peace, so that your believing lives, filled with the life-giving energy of the Holy Spirit, will brim over with hope!

Romans 15:13 MSG

Having hope can be a major destressor. It's about putting your worries aside and focusing on what *could* be. That doesn't mean you take a dreamy stance, just wondering what will happen next while you wait on the sidelines. What it does mean is taking some kind of action, giving all you can, doing all you can, to make that hope a reality. But at the same time, you're to put the entire situation, person, problem, issue into God's hands. For in *Him* is your true hope. Because no matter what happens, you trust in the One who has your best interests at heart, the One who knows all, the One who sees beyond what you see, the One who will do what is best for His world, His people, His planet.

Stress Less, Pray More

We must always be on the lookout for the weak, the heavy-laden, and the downcast. Let us help them with their burdens, anxieties, fears, and questionings—imparting to them something of our cheery hope. . . .

We must fulfill the injunctions of Romans 15:9–13, rejoicing in praise and abounding in hope. The outlook on the earth-side may be dark and depressing, but uncurtain your windows toward God—see, the land is light.

F. B. MEYER, *Bible Commentary*

Gaining Sweet Peace

Trust in the LORD with all your heart and do not lean on your own understanding. In all your ways acknowledge Him, and He will make your paths straight.

PROVERBS 3:5–6 NASB

When it comes to making decisions, we tend to ask the advice of others. After weighing all the answers we've received, we then do what seems right to us. Many times afterward, we find ourselves going down the wrong path. Or asking God to change the results. Meanwhile, He's waiting for us to petition Him for wisdom and trust what He advises, no matter how outlandish it may seem. For only when we trust God with all our heart and leave all decisions to Him do we find the right path. Only then do we find true peace of heart and mind.

Study to follow His will in all, to have no will but His. This is thy duty, and thy wisdom. Nothing is gained by spurning and struggling but to hurt and vex thyself; but by complying all is gained—sweet peace. It is the very secret, the mystery of solid peace within, to resign all to His will, to be disposed of at His pleasure, without the least contrary thought.

ROBERT LEIGHTON

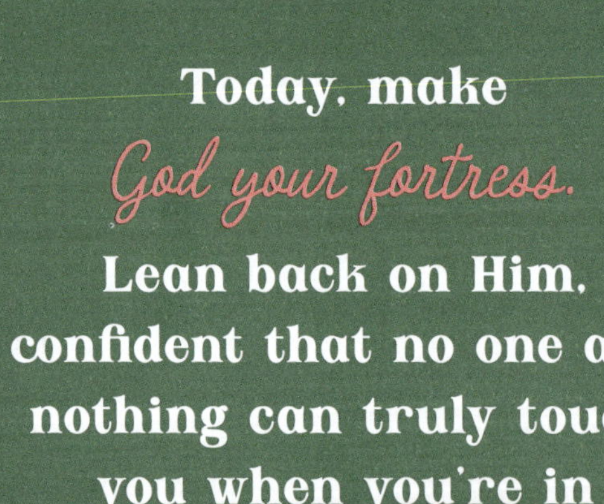

Today, make

God your fortress.

Lean back on Him, confident that no one and nothing can truly touch you when you're in

His presence.

Sheltered in the Peace of God

He who dwells in the secret place of the Most High shall remain stable and fixed under the shadow of the Almighty [Whose power no foe can withstand]. I will say of the Lord, He is my Refuge and my Fortress, my God; on Him I lean and rely, and in Him I [confidently] trust!

PSALM 91:1–2 AMPC

How wonderful to dwell in the secret place with the Most High. A place where you can find the peace your soul and spirit crave. For there is no greater calm than that found when you take refuge under the shadow of the Supreme Being "Whose power no foe can withstand"!

Today, make God your fortress. Lean back on Him, confident that no one and nothing can truly touch you when you're in His presence.

To those who are His, all things are not only easy to be borne, but even to be gladly chosen. Their will is united to that will which moves heaven and earth, which gives laws to angels, and rules the courses of the world. It is a wonderful gift of God to man, of which we that know so little must needs speak little. To be at the center of that motion, where is everlasting rest; to be sheltered in the peace of God; even now to dwell in heaven, where all hearts are stayed, and all hopes fulfilled. "Thou shalt keep him in perfect peace whose mind is stayed on Thee" [Isaiah 26:3].

HENRY EDWARD MANNING

Peace Like a Gentle River

"I am the Lord your God, who teaches you what is good for you and leads you along the paths you should follow. Oh, that you had listened to my commands! Then you would have had peace flowing like a gentle river and righteousness rolling over you like waves in the sea."

Isaiah 48:17–18 NLT

When things are going well in our lives, chances are it's because we are obeying the sole Being who knows what is good for us. And that Being is God. When we follow where He leads, when we listen to Him when He whispers in our ears, "This is the way you should go" (Isaiah 30:21 NLT), we find the peace we have been searching for.

Today, consider how much peace there is in your life. If you're finding it elusive at best, go to God in prayer. Ask Him to tell you the way you should go. Then follow His directions, "whether to the right or to the left" (Isaiah 30:21 NLT).

My Lord, I find that nothing else will do,
But follow where thou goest, sit at thy feet,
And where I have thee not, still run to meet.
Roses are scentless, hopeless are the morns,
Rest is but weakness, laughter crackling thorns,
If thou, the Truth, do not make them the true:
Thou art my life, O Christ, and nothing else will do.

George MacDonald

No Quaking Here

Though the mountains should depart and the hills be shaken or removed, yet My love and kindness shall not depart from you, nor shall My covenant of peace and completeness be removed, says the Lord, Who has compassion on you. . . .Therefore we will not fear, though the earth should change and though the mountains be shaken into the midst of the seas.

Isaiah 54:10; Psalm 46:2 AMPC

The world has been shaking things up lately as the weather becomes more and more extreme, and unprecedented weather patterns are now commonplace. So it's no wonder we ourselves feel a little bit shaky. After all, we don't know what to expect next!

It's hard to find a place of peace when the ground beneath you is shaking and the waters around you are rising. Thank God we have God! No matter what happens with Mother Earth, no matter how strange the weather might become, we need not fear but rest ourselves in God whose peace will never depart from us—unless we let it.

So today, keep your peace. And, if you've got some time, maybe clean up a river.

Christ is the pledge that I shall one day see;
That one day, still with him, I shall awake,
And know my God, at one with him and free.
O lordly essence, come to life in me;
The will-throb let me feel that doth me make;
Now have I many a mighty hope in thee,
Then shall I rest although the universe should quake.

George MacDonald

Mounting Up

Sing and make music to the Lord with your hearts.

EPHESIANS 5:19 GW

We are commanded to have our hearts filled with songs of rejoicing and to make inward melody to the Lord. But unless we mount up with wings this is impossible, for the only creature that can sing is the creature that flies. When the prophet declared that though all the world should be desolate, yet he would rejoice in God and joy in the God of his salvation, his soul was surely on wings. Paul knew what it was to use his wings when he found himself to be "sorrowful, yet always rejoicing." On the earthly plane all was dark to both Paul and the prophet, but on the heavenly plane all was brightest sunshine.

Do you know anything of this life on wings, dear reader? Do you "mount up" continually to God, out of and above earth's cares and trials, to that higher plane of life where all is peace and triumph? . . .

Do you think that by flying I mean necessarily any very joyous emotions or feelings of exhilaration. . . ? The flying I mean is a matter of *principle*, not a matter of *emotion*. It may be accompanied by very joyous emotions, but it does not depend on them. It depends only upon the facts of an entire surrender and an absolute trust. Every one who will honestly use these two wings and will faithfully persist in using them, will find that they *have* mounted up with wings as an eagle.

HANNAH WHITALL SMITH, *The Christian's Secret of a Happy Life*

Come Away!

His left hand is under my head, and his right hand embraces me! . . . My beloved speaks and says to me: "Arise, my love, my beautiful one, and come away."

Song of Solomon 2:6, 10 esv

God longs to have an intimate relationship with you. He doesn't want your worries about what may or may not happen to become a barrier between you, to distract you from what He can do and is doing in your life. To tear down the wall of worry, find a quiet place. Tell God all that's on your mind. Relax as you imagine God right next to you. Say, "[I can feel] his left hand under my head and his right hand embraces me!" (Song of Solomon 2:6 AMPC). Spend as much time as you'd like with Him, enjoying His presence, listening for His voice, hearing what He has to say. Then arise, beautiful one, and go with Him wherever He leads.

Today, pray: Lord of all, my Beloved, I can feel Your left hand beneath my head, Your right hand embracing me. Let me rest in this peace, surrounded by Your presence and love. And then, as I arise with You, stay by my side as I walk in peace with You. Amen.

Worry Less, Pray More

No sooner did I cry out for help, but he was at hand to succour me, and did manifest his tender care and dear love to me.

Matthew Poole's Commentary

It's All Good

"You meant evil against me, but God meant it for good."
. . .Though I walk in the midst of trouble, you preserve
my life. . . . The Lord will fulfill his purpose for me.

Genesis 50:20; Psalm 138:7–8 esv

There may be people in our lives like Joseph's brothers in the Old Testament. They plot evil against us, lay traps before us, or sell us out. Yet no matter what happens, God can make that evil done against us work out for good.

So instead of losing our peace amid trouble, why not follow the ways of Joseph? No matter what or who came against him, he trusted in God. And because he did so, the Lord was with him and made him and everything he did successful (Genesis 39:2, 5, 21, 23). God also helped Joseph forget all the hardships he suffered and made him fruitful (Genesis 41:51–52).

Chances are, if Joseph had only moaned and groaned about his circumstances, he would've quickly succumbed to depression or despair. After all, he was sold to foreigners, taken from his home, accused of a rape he didn't commit, and left almost totally forgotten in a dungeon! But as Joseph kept trusting God, God kept blessing him, ultimately making him second only to the pharaoh in Egypt.

No matter what happens, keep your faith and peace as you put complete trust in God, knowing He'll stick with you and make all things work out for good.

A Settled Peace

My soul, wait thou only upon God; for my expectation is from him. He only is my rock and my salvation: he is my defence; I shall not be moved.

PSALM 62:5–6 KJV

Today's prayer shows you the peace that can settle upon you when you leave all your expectations in God's hands—when you keep in mind that all that happens is according to His good plan, one so much better than anything you can imagine. Pray. Experience the freedom gained when you leave all you have and are to the Master.

365 Devotions on the Power of Prayer

O Lord, Who hast breathed into me the breath of life, and endued me with an immortal spirit, which looks up unto Thee, and remembers it is made after Thine own image, behold with grace and favor the ardent desires which are in my heart, to recover a perfect likeness of Thee. Endue me with more contentedness in what is present, and less solicitude about what is future; with a patient mind to submit to any loss of what I have, or any disappointment of what I expect. Fill me, O Lord, with the knowledge of Thy will, in all wisdom and spiritual understanding. Fill me with goodness, and the fruits of righteousness. And fill me with all joy and peace in believing that Thou wilt never leave me nor forsake me, but make me perfect, stablish, strengthen, settle me, and be my God for ever and ever; my Guide unto death. Amen.

SIMON PATRICK

The Master of Perfection

And let the beauty and delightfulness and favor of the Lord our God be upon us; confirm and establish the work of our hands—yes, the work of our hands, confirm and establish it.

Psalm 90:17 AMPC

Probably we have heard the sermon illustration about the wearied and discouraged young artist who put his head down on the table and slept beside the oil painting he had struggled over for weeks. No one could accuse him of not giving the work his best try. He had poured all the talent that he had into the picture.

While the artist slept, his painting master quietly entered the room and went to the sleeping boy, picked up a brush, and with his skilled hands began painting. With just a few touches, the beauty that had eluded the young artist began to appear. In just a few minutes the canvas became all that the young artist wanted it to be.

While that kind of teaching may be questionable, many of us need to be reminded that when we are tired and spent and lay down whatever our toiling might be, our own great Master will make perfect our endeavors for Him. From our service He will remove every stain, every blemish, and every failure. To our service He will give the brightest luster and highest honor. Shall we not bring ourselves to the One who can make us better?

William "Billy" Sunday

The Place of Peace

I am continually with You; You do hold my right hand. You will guide me with Your counsel, and afterward receive me to honor and glory. . . . My flesh and my heart may fail, but God is the Rock and firm Strength of my heart and my Portion forever. . . . It is good for me to draw near to God; I have put my trust in the Lord God and made Him my refuge.

PSALM 73:23–24, 26, 28 AMPC

There you are, walking along with God, riding the ups and downs with Him. And then you turn and see someone traveling the road of life. But this person is evil, downright wicked in what he says and does. Yet he seems to have the life you've always wanted. He doesn't worry about money, lives in a nice home, and has beautiful children—the seemingly perfect life!

And then you enter into God's presence. You step into His sanctuary of peace and goodness. And you realize that those who are evil will soon be wiped away, never remembered, bankrupt of more than just their riches.

You, woman of God, are in the right place, living the right life. There may be some rough spots as you walk with God, but He'll be with you through both good and not-so-good times. He'll give you the peace and security you need. So on those tough days, just draw near to God. Put your trust in Him. And He'll give you all the refuge you need and take you to that unsurpassable place of peace.

The Legacy of Peace

"Peace I leave with you. My peace I give to you. I do not give to you as the world gives."

JOHN 14:27 HCSB

How we treasure the last sayings of a dying parent! How specially cherished and memorable are his last looks and last words. This text is the last words—the parting legacy—of a dying Savior. It is a legacy of peace.

How different from the false and counterfeit peace in which so many are content to live and content to die. The world's peace is all well, so long as prosperity lasts, so long as the stream runs smoothly and the sky is clear; but when the flood is at hand or the storm is gathering, where is the world's peace? It is gone! There is no calculating on its permanency. Often when the cup is fullest, there is the trembling apprehension that in one brief moment it may be dashed to the ground. The soul may be saying to itself, "Peace, peace," but like the drawing in the sand, it may be obliterated by the first wave of adversity.

But, "not as the world gives!" The peace of the believer is deep, calm, lasting, everlasting. The world, with all its blandishments, cannot give it. The world, with all its vicissitudes and fluctuations, cannot take it away. It is the brightest in the hour of trial; it lights up the final valley-like gloom.

JOHN MACDUFF

The Way of Peace

The dayspring from on high hath visited us, to give light to them that sit in darkness and in the shadow of death, to guide our feet into the way of peace.

LUKE 1:78–79 KJV

God's light follows you everywhere you go, giving you rest whenever and wherever you need it. Secure in His presence, you know you need not fear at night. As you close your eyes, you know He is with you, guarding you as you sleep. If you awaken during the night, He will be there to soothe you, to give you ease of mind and heart. And when you awaken to a new day, you turn to His presence once again, to Jesus your sun, the Spirit your comforter. With the Holy Three in your midst, you find the eagerness to face the tasks before you, the strength to meet whatever comes, and the guidance that leads you in the path of peace. Pray today for the rest you find in God alone.

365 Devotions on the Power of Prayer

Go with each of us to rest; if any awake, temper them the dark hours of watching; and when the day returns, return to us, our sun and comforter, and call us up with morning faces and with morning hearts, eager to labour, eager to be happy, if happiness should be our portion, and if the day be marked for sorrow, strong to endure it. Amen.

ROBERT LOUIS STEVENSON

No Lack

The Lord is my Shepherd [to feed, guide, and shield me], I shall not lack. He makes me lie down in [fresh, tender] green pastures; He leads me beside the still and restful waters. He refreshes and restores my life (my self).

Psalm 23:1–3 AMPC

We're satisfied with what we have—until the next new shiny thing comes out and is dangled before our eyes. Then we're suddenly unsettled, unable to rest until we have it in our hands, only to have it too soon lose its luster and be placed in a closet, junk drawer, storage unit, or thrift shop.

Break the chain of want. Realize that God has everything you need. With Him to feed, guide, and shield you, you will never lack. And you will find peace in mind, heart, and hand.

Who is it that is your shepherd? The Lord! Oh, my friends, what a wonderful announcement! The Lord God of heaven and earth, the almighty Creator of all things, He who holds the universe in His hand as though it were a very little thing—*He* is your shepherd, and has charged Himself with the care and keeping of you, as a shepherd is charged with the care and keeping of his sheep. If your hearts could really take in this thought, you would never have a fear or a care again; for with such a shepherd, how could it be possible for you ever to want any good thing?

HANNAH WHITALL SMITH

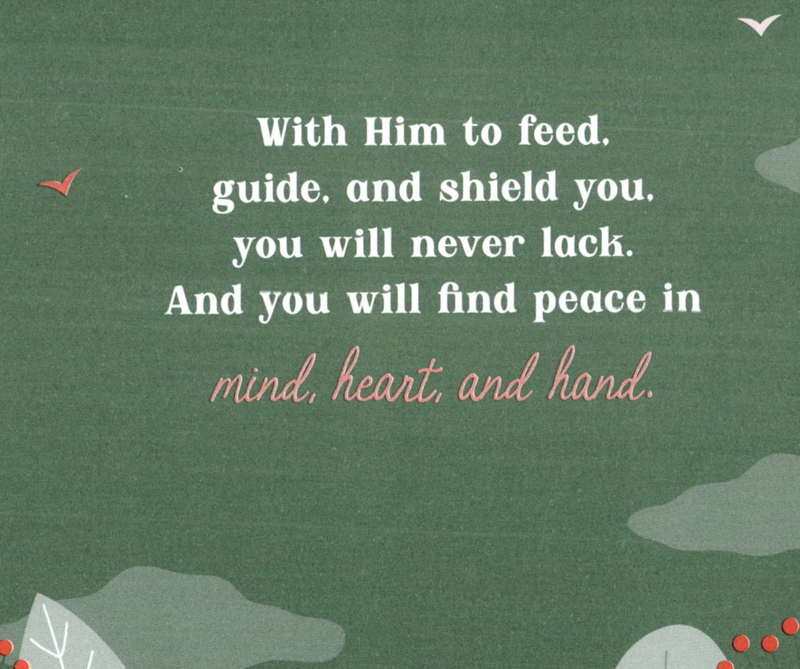

With Him to feed,
guide, and shield you,
you will never lack.
And you will find peace in
mind, heart, and hand.

One Thing Needful

Martha was cumbered about much serving, and came to him, and said, Lord, dost thou not care that my sister hath left me to serve alone? bid her therefore that she help me. And Jesus answered and said unto her, Martha, Martha, thou art careful and troubled about many things: but one thing is needful: and Mary hath chosen that good part, which shall not be taken away from her.

LUKE 10:40–42 KJV

Is your doing for God making you fretful? Or are you at His feet, simply listening, finding His peace along with His guidance?

There is no evidence that Martha had a worldly or covetous disposition. Her anxiety was to provide suitable entertainment for the Lord Jesus. As mistress of the family, this care properly devolved on her; and the only fault which can be charged on her was too earnest a desire to make such entertainment, when she might have sat with Mary at his feet, and, perhaps, too much haste and fretfulness in speaking to Jesus about Mary.

Barnes' Notes on the Bible

He who had welcomed the crowds was now welcomed for His own dear sake. Martha and Mary each gave of her best. Each had her own sphere; one ministered to His physical need, the other to His heart. The mystical and practical are both required in Christ's service, and blend at His feet. Don't live for many things; but for Him.

F. B. MEYER, *Bible Commentary*

The Peace of Love

Dear friends, let us love one another.

1 John 4:7 NIV

Wouldst thou overcome the world? Let Christ enter, and the world will have no charms for thee. There is only one source of pure, divine love, and wherever that love is present you know that the possessor has found its source in God. God's love is absolutely selfless. He loves the unloving to make them love, putting away their sin, and perfecting their union with himself.

F. B. MEYER, *Bible Commentary*

Nothing is sweeter than love, nothing more courageous, nothing higher, nothing wider, nothing more pleasant, nothing fuller nor better in heaven and earth, because love is born of God, and cannot rest but in God, above all created things.

Love feels no burden, thinks nothing of trouble, attempts what is above its strength, pleads no excuse of impossibility. It is therefore able to undertake all things, and it completes many things and warrants them to take effect, where he who does not love would faint and lie down. Love is watchful and sleeping, slumbering not. Though weary, it is not tired; though pressed, it is not straitened; though alarmed, it is not confounded; but, as a lively flame and burning torch, it forces its way upward and securely passes all.

Three men are my friends—he that loves me, he that hates me, he that is indifferent to me. Who loves me teaches me tenderness; who hates me teaches me caution; who is indifferent to me teaches me self-reliance.

THOMAS À KEMPIS

Peace-Provoking Truths

My sheep hear my voice, and I know them, and they follow me: and I give unto them eternal life; and they shall never perish, neither shall any man pluck them out of my hand. My Father, which gave them me, is greater than all; and no man is able to pluck them out of my Father's hand.

JOHN 10:27–29 KJV

How wonderful that we can hear our Lord's voice. That He knows each one of us. That we cannot help but follow Him. That we will never perish, nor be plucked out of God's hand. May these peace-provoking truths be seared on our souls.

It is true that, looking forward, there may be long avenues of tribulation, but the glory is at the end of them; battles may be foreseen, and woe to the person who does not expect them, but the eye of faith perceives the crown of victory. Deep waters are mapped upon our journey, but faith can see Jehovah fording these rivers with us, and she anticipates the day when we shall ascend the banks of the shore and enter into Jehovah's rest.

When we have received these priceless truths into our souls, we are satisfied with favor and full of the goodness of the Lord. I value the gospel not only for what it has done for me in the past, but for the guarantees which it affords me of eternal salvation. "I give unto them eternal life; and they shall never perish, neither shall any man pluck them out of my hand."

CHARLES SPURGEON

Rich in Peace

"Peace I leave with you; my peace I give you.
I do not give to you as the world gives."
JOHN 14:27 NIV

"You will keep him in perfect peace, whose mind is stayed on You" (Isaiah 26:3 NKJV). "Perfect peace"—what a blessed attainment. Dear reader, is it yours? Do you have the sense of hope that peace brings about?

If you have all that the world calls enviable and happy, unless you have peace in God and with God, all else is unworthy of the name. Perfect peace! What is it? It is the peace of forgiveness. It is the peace arising out of a sense of God reconciled through the blood of the everlasting covenant—resting on the bosom and work of Jesus.

My soul, stay yourself on God, so that this blessed peace may be yours. You have tried the world. It has deceived you. Prop after prop of earthly scaffolding has yielded and tottered and fallen. Has our God ever done that? False and counterfeit world peace may do well for the world's work and worldly prosperity. But test it in the hour of sorrow—what can it do for you when it is most needed?

On the other hand, even if you have no other blessing on the earth to call your own, you are rich indeed if you can look up to heaven and say with a smile, "I am at peace with God."

JOHN MACDUFF

Peace at the Last

And I heard a voice from heaven saying unto me, Write, Blessed are the dead which die in the Lord from henceforth: Yea, saith the Spirit, that they may rest from their labours; and their works do follow them.

REVELATION 14:13 KJV

One of the great things about being a God follower is that whether you're alive or dead, Christ is with you. Because He's "Lord both of the dead and living" (Romans 14:9)! So, while you're here, God the Father will support you, hold you up, strengthen you, imbue you with power—whatever needs to be given to keep you walking His way. And then, when your work here is done, Jesus will meet you at the gates of heaven where God the Father already has a place prepared for you, one that's safe, where you can rest in peace at last.

So no worries. Keep following God. Pray for His help while you're in the sun today and for His haven in heaven when your earthly days are done!

365 Devotions on the Power of Prayer

O Father, support me all the day long of this troublous life, until the shadows lengthen, and the evening comes, and the busy world is hushed, and the fever of life is over, and my work is done. Then, dear Father, in Thy mercy grant me a safe lodging, a holy rest, and a peace at the last; through Jesus Christ, Thy Son and my Lord. Amen.

JOHN HENRY NEWMAN

A Home Builder

A wise woman builds her home, but a foolish woman tears it down with her own hands.

Proverbs 14:1 NLT

Worry has a domino effect. If you start fretting over something that has caught your attention and then voice it or act panic-stricken, chances are others around you will fall in with your anxiety. Everyone in your household, church, or workplace will come unglued. Better to be a wise woman who builds up her home and her fellow travelers with a steady life of prayer and encouragement as well as an evident faith in God.

When worries enter your thoughts, seek Jesus' face immediately. Ask Him to take on your troubles as you pick up His peace. Trust that He will see you through no matter what lies ahead or behind. Then you will be in a position to help others work through their own worries, mostly by being a calm, good listener, encouraging them when they need it, and giving wise advice when asked.

May you pray: Lord, help me be a wise woman, building up my home by giving You my worries and taking on Your peace.

Worry Less, Pray More

Worry is not about the possible troubles of the future; for if they come, you are but anticipating and adding to their weight; and if they do not come, your worry is useless; and in either case, it is weak and in vain, and a distrust of God's providence.

HUGH BLAIR

A Curious Peace

As many as walk according to this rule, peace be on them, and mercy, and upon the Israel of God.

GALATIANS 6:16 KJV

There is a wonderful and curious peace experienced when we put our day, our work, and ourselves in God's hands. May you obtain that peace today and every day.

Lord, I have given my life to Thee,
And every day and hour is Thine—
What Thou appointest let them be;
Thy will is better, Lord, than mine.

ANNA B. WARNER

Begin at once; before you venture away from this quiet moment, ask your King to take you wholly into His service, and place all the hours of this day quite simply at His disposal, and ask Him to make and keep you ready to do just exactly what He appoints. Never mind about tomorrow; one day at a time is enough. Try it today, and see if it is not a day of strange, almost curious peace, so sweet that you will be only too thankful, when tomorrow comes, to ask Him to take it also—till it will become a blessed habit to hold yourself simply and "wholly at Thy commandment for any manner of service" [1 Chronicles 28:21]. The "whatsoever" is not necessarily active work. It may be waiting (whether half an hour or half a lifetime), learning, suffering, sitting still. But shall we be less ready for these, if any of them are His appointments for today? Let us ask Him to prepare us for all that He is preparing for us.

FRANCES RIDLEY HAVERGAL

For God Alone

For God alone my soul waits in silence; from him comes my salvation. . . . For God alone, O my soul, wait in silence, for my hope is from him. He only is my rock and my salvation, my fortress; I shall not be shaken. . . . Trust in him at all times. . . ; pour out your heart before him; God is a refuge for us.

PSALM 62:1, 5–6, 8 ESV

When stress comes knocking at your door, remember to breathe. Then calm your heart by reminding your soul to wait in silence. Remember your hope is in God alone. He's the one thing you can stand tall on, the unchangeable, the solid rock. He's the One who saves you—over and over again. He's the One you can run to, the One who's always there for you. With God in your life, nothing can shake you up. Breathe.

Then pour your heart out to the One you trust. The One who protects you, who's your ultimate shelter in the storm *and* the sun. He's waiting.

Today, simply pray: I'm coming to You, Lord, for peace, for assurance, for help, for sanctuary, for love.

Stress Less, Pray More

There are times when God seems so near that we cannot speak aloud, but are just silent before Him and breathe out our thoughts and desires.

F. B. MEYER, *Bible Commentary*

Be still silent, O my soul! submit thyself completely, trust immovably, wait patiently.

CHARLES SPURGEON, *The Treasury of David*

Grasp the Peace

Let this mind be in you, which was also in Christ Jesus: who, being in the form of God, thought it not robbery to be equal with God: but made himself of no reputation, and took upon him the form of a servant, and was made in the likeness of men: and being found in fashion as a man, he humbled himself, and became obedient.

PHILIPPIANS 2:5–8 KJV

God has formed you into the person you are now, the one reading these words. He has certain tasks He wants you to perform. He has a mission, duties, for you in this generation—to live as an example to others, shed your light, love and forgive all, be like Christ. But God needs some help.

God needs you to be willing. He needs you to be pliant, to bend to His will. That means not getting caught up in your own desires. Not letting fear rule over you. Not having a worldly mind-set. God wants you to give Him total control. To acknowledge that Christ rules your heart—and then let Him do it! To refer all things to the wisdom of the Holy Spirit within. To be humble and obedient.

And that's what today's four-word prayer is all about. Being humble and obedient, giving yourself up to God's will. To have that mind of Christ in you. And, in so doing, grasp the courage, peace, strength, and power that go with it!

365 Devotions on the Power of Prayer

Oh, Lord, bend me!

EVAN ROBERTS

Reposing in the Present

Consider the lilies of the field, how they grow.

MATTHEW 6:28 KJV

Surely these words give us the picture of a life and growth far different from the ordinary life and growth of Christians—a life of rest and a growth without effort. . . .

We may rest assured of this, that all the resources of God's infinite grace will be brought to bear on the growing of the tiniest flower in His spiritual garden as certainly as they are in His earthly creation; and as the violet abides peacefully in its little place, content to receive its daily portion without concerning itself about the wandering of the winds or the falling of the rain, so must we repose in the present moment as it comes to us from God, contented with our daily portion and without anxious thought as to anything that may be whirling around us in God's glorious universe, sure that all things will be made to "prosper" for us.

This is the kind of "growth in grace" in which we who have entered into the life of full trust, believe; a growth without care or anxiety on our part, but a growth which does actually grow, which blossoms out into flower and fruit and becomes like a "tree planted by the rivers of water, that bringeth forth his fruit in his season"; whose leaf also does not wither, and who prospers in whatsoever he doeth.

HANNAH WHITALL SMITH, *The Christian's Secret of a Happy Life*

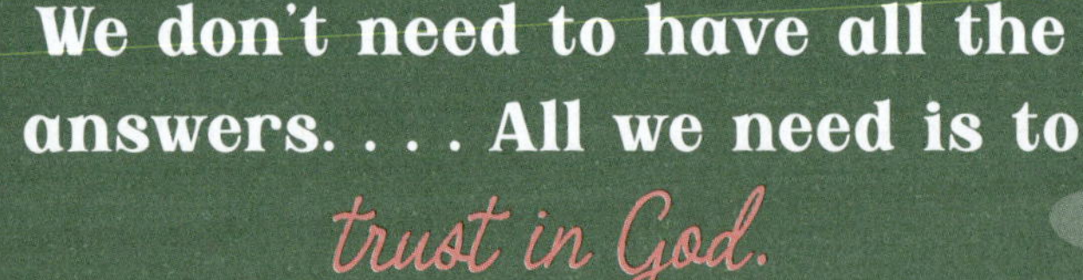

We don't need to have all the answers. . . . All we need is to *trust in God.*

Find our peace in Him.
And know that by living in
His world and according
to His Word, all things,
including us, will prosper.

Calm and Unmoved

Oh, the joys of those who. . .delight in the law of the LORD, meditating on it day and night. They are like trees planted along the riverbank, bearing fruit each season. Their leaves never wither, and they prosper in all they do. . . . LORD, my heart is not proud, nor my eyes arrogant; nor do I involve myself in great matters, or in things too difficult for me.

PSALM 1:1–3 NLT; PSALM 131:1 NASB

There are some things we may never understand. We may never comprehend how certain events and experiences connect to our lives. And that's okay. We don't need to have all the answers, to know all the whys and wherefores. All we need is to trust in God. Find our peace in Him. And know that by living in His world and according to His Word, all things, including us, will prosper.

My mind is forever closed against embarrassment and perplexity, against uncertainty, doubt, and anxiety; my heart against grief and desire. Calm and unmoved, I look down on all things, for I know that I cannot explain a single event, nor comprehend its connection with that which alone concerns me. In His world all things prosper; this satisfies me, and in this belief I stand fast as a rock. My breast is steeled against annoyance on account of personal offences and vexations, or exultation in personal merit; for my whole personality has disappeared in the contemplation of the purpose of my being.

JOHANN G. FICHTE

Let Love and Peace Enter

Be perfect, be of good comfort, be of one mind, live in peace; and the God of love and peace shall be with you. . . . The grace of the Lord Jesus Christ, and the love of God, and the communion of the Holy Ghost, be with you all. Amen.

2 Corinthians 13:11, 14 kjv

The secret to living in peace? "Be joyful. Grow to maturity. Encourage each other. Live in harmony and peace. Then the God of love and peace will be with you" (2 Corinthians 13:11 nlt). It's that easy.

"Be perfect," v. 11, is really "be adjusted," "properly jointed," "articulated." God desires to set us as a skillful surgeon sets a dislocated limb. Let Him do it; let the Comforter comfort; let love and peace enter with the Holy Dove; and see that the inner atmosphere does not hinder the gracious healing work of the Spirit of God.

Note the threefold benediction, which maintains the doctrine of the Trinity, v. 14. The love of the Father is the fountain of all; the grace of the Lord Jesus is the channel for all; while the communion of the Holy Spirit brings us into partnership with the aims and resources of God.

F. B. MEYER, *Bible Commentary*

God is the Author of peace and Lover of concord; he hath loved us, and is willing to be at peace with us. And let it be our constant aim so to walk.

Matthew Henry's Commentary

Truth

Jesus said, "I am the Road, also the Truth, also the Life. No one gets to the Father apart from me. If you really knew me, you would know my Father as well. From now on, you do know him. You've even seen him!"

John 14:6–7 msg

In this world of "fake news" where we are surrounded by so much misinformation, it's so reassuring to delve into the truth of God's Word written thousands of years ago, wisdom that has stood the test of time. How comforting and amazing that we have access to and can follow the Word that reveals God the Father to us, helping us to know Him and what He would have us do.

Keep the truth, wisdom, and knowledge the Bible provides close to your heart. Write it on the walls of your mind. Cling to it amid trials and you'll find a peace that surpasses all understanding. Stay on the Road, stick to the Truth, and you'll be living the Life God has planned for you and those you love.

Stress Less, Pray More

Christ is the sinner's Way to the Father and to heaven. . . . He is the Life, by whose life-giving Spirit the dead in sin are quickened. Nor can any man draw nigh God as a Father, who is not. . .taught by Him as the Truth, to come by Him as the Way. By Christ, as the Way, our prayers go to God, and His blessings come to us; this is the Way that leads to rest, the good old Way.

Matthew Henry's Concise Commentary

The Peace Beyond

And the city had no need of the sun, neither of the moon, to shine in it: for the glory of God did lighten it, and the Lamb is the light thereof. . . . And the gates of it shall not be shut at all by day: for there shall be no night there.

REVELATION 21:23, 25 KJV

Today's wonders of the sky and earth are but a poor reflection of the new heaven and earth that await you. A place where you will dwell in peace. Where the only light will be that of Christ. Where there will be no noise or silence but the music of angels. Where there will be no fear or hope but all things shared. Where there will be no beginning or end but a glorious eternity in a heavenly world without end.

As you pray today, ask God to bring you there in that glorious day. And to keep that vision in your mind, spirit, and heart as you face the hours before you.

365 Devotions on the Power of Prayer

Bring us, O Lord God, at our last awakening into the house and gate of heaven to enter into that gate and dwell in that house, where there shall be no darkness nor dazzling, but one equal light; no noise nor silence, but one equal music; no fears nor hopes, but one equal possession; no ends nor beginnings, but one equal eternity; in the habitations of thy glory and dominion, world without end.

JOHN DONNE

Waiting upon the Lord

They that wait upon the L*ORD shall renew their strength; they shall mount up with wings as eagles; they shall run, and not be weary; and they shall walk, and not faint.*

Isaiah 40:31 KJV

Often, where there is no conscious sin the soul is still unconsciously tethered to something of earth and so struggles in vain to fly. A party of my friends once got into a boat in Norway to row around one of the fiords there. They took their seats and began to row vigorously, but the boat made no headway. They put out more strength and rowed harder than before, but all in vain; not an inch did the boat move. Then one of the party suddenly recollected that the boat had not been unmoored, and he exclaimed, "No wonder we could not get away, when we were trying to pull the whole continent of Europe after us!" And just so our souls are often not unmoored from earthly things. We must cut ourselves loose. As well might an eagle try to fly with a hundred-ton weight tied fast to its feet, as the soul try to "mount up with wings" while a weight of earthly cares and anxieties is holding it down to earth. . . .

The promise is sure: "They that wait upon the Lord *shall* mount up with wings as eagles." Not "may perhaps mount up," but *"shall."* It is the inevitable result. May we each one prove it for ourselves!

HANNAH WHITALL SMITH, *The Christian's Secret of a Happy Life*

Free and Endless Refills

Ever be filled and stimulated with the [Holy] Spirit.

Ephesians 5:18 AMPC

In this world there are many things you can turn to to fulfill yourself, to satisfy your cravings for energy, strength, even peace. Turning to the world's salve can lead to even more stress. But God would have you turn to Him. For being filled with Him and His Spirit is not a once and done thing, happening only when you profess your belief in your big Brother Jesus. It's a continual refilling.

So turn to God. Recognize the fact that "you are God's temple and that God's Spirit dwells in you" (1 Corinthians 3:16 ESV). Daily pray for God to refresh you deep within, taking into account that "if you. . .know how to give good gifts [gifts that are to their advantage] to your children, how much more will your heavenly Father give the Holy Spirit to those who ask and continue to ask Him!" (Luke 11:13 AMPC).

Stress Less, Pray More

Learn but in quietness and stillness to retire to the Lord, and wait upon Him; in whom thou shall feel peace and joy, in the midst of thy trouble from the cruel and vexatious spirit of this world. So wait to know thy work and service to the Lord every day, in thy place and station; and the Lord make thee faithful therein, and thou wilt want neither help, support, nor comfort.

ISAAC PENINGTON

A Catching Calm

If I were still trying to please man, I would not be a servant of Christ.

GALATIANS 1:10 ESV

When we spend our days practicing God's presence, we find ourselves imitating Christ, living and working calmly. And it's exactly that kind of calm that is catching.

As Brother Lawrence has found such an advantage in walking in the presence of God, it is natural for him to recommend it earnestly to others—to those who have lost all hope for personal devotion—but his example is a stronger inducement than any arguments he could propose.

His very countenance is edifying; such a sweet and calm devotion appearing in it, as could not but affect the beholders. And it is observed, that in the greatest hurry of business in the kitchen, he still preserves his heavenly-mindedness. He is never hasty nor loitering, but he does each thing in its season, with an even uninterrupted composure and tranquility of spirit; he says, "To me the time of business does not differ from the time of prayer; and in the noise and clatter of my kitchen while several brothers are at the same time calling for my attention, I possess God in as great tranquility as if I were upon my knees at the Sacrament.

"The most excellent method I have of going to God is in doing my common business without any view of pleasing men. My hope of glory is found in performing purely for the love of God."

BROTHER LAWRENCE AND HIS INTERVIEWER

In Christ's Spirit

Be likeminded, . . .being of. . .one mind. . . .
Let this mind be in you, which was also in Christ Jesus.
PHILIPPIANS 2:2, 5 KJV

To be in Christ is to live out His ideas, character, and spirit as the atmosphere of your being. People everywhere are living out the ideas and character of others. He who lives in the spirit of Raphael becomes a painter; he who lives in the spirit of Milton becomes a poet; he who lives in the spirit of Bacon becomes a philosopher; he who lives in the spirit of Caesar becomes a warrior. He who lives in the spirit of Jesus Christ becomes a mature person.

In the spirit of Christ, live for something outside of yourself. Do good and leave behind you a monument of virtue that the storm of time can never destroy. Write your name in kindness, love, and mercy on the hearts of thousands you come in contact with year by year; you will never be forgotten. No, your name, your deeds, will be as legible on the hearts you leave behind as the stars on the brow of evening. Good deeds will shine as the star of heaven.

Is life worth living? Yes, so long as there is wrong to right, so long as lingers gloom to chase or streaming tears to dry, so long as a tale of anguish swells the heart and eyes grow wet and, at the sound of God's Word, we pardon and forget. Is life worth living? Only when we are living in Christ and let Him shine through us.

THOMAS CHALMERS

God Moves

Their cry. . .ascended to God. And God heard their sighing and groaning and [earnestly] remembered His covenant. . . . God saw the Israelites and took knowledge of them and concerned Himself about them [knowing all, understanding, remembering all].

Exodus 2:23–25 AMPC

Some time after Joseph died, a new pharaoh came into power—not knowing or remembering what Joseph had done for Egypt and its people. By this time, the Israelites had become very well off. And they had rapidly and greatly multiplied in number.

Thus, the new pharaoh, feeling threatened, decided to enslave the Hebrew population. He did so with hopes that the overworked and overburdened Israelites would never threaten him with their numbers.

Yet when God's people cried out to Him, when their pleas reached His ears, God heard. God remembered. God saw. God understood. And God moved. He took swift action—beginning with two Hebrew midwives who found the courage to disobey Pharaoh's edict to kill boys at birth. And then He raised up, educated, prepared, and trained a new leader by the name of Moses.

You too are one of God's people. When you are under pressure, in deep trouble, cry out to God. Know that God will hear. God will remember. God will see. God will understand. God will move on your behalf, will give you victory no matter what the odds, and will make a way where there seems to be no way.

Take a Breath

[It is] the Spirit of God that made me [which has stirred me up], and the breath of the Almighty that gives me life [which inspires me].

Job 33:4 AMPC

What do you do when the flight, fight, or freeze button has been pushed and stress has taken over? When you can't seem to get your bearings and need a way to just calm down?

No matter where you are or when, hit the PAUSE button. Become aware of what's going on mentally, physically, spiritually, and emotionally. Remind yourself that God is with you. Then, through several deep belly breaths, reconnect with the source of all creation.

Link up with the God who breathed life into you, as He did Adam: "The LORD God formed man of the dust of the ground, and breathed into his nostrils the breath of life; and man became a living being" (Genesis 2:7 NKJV). Find your way back into Jesus, who breathed the Word of life into His followers: "When He had said this, He breathed on them, and said to them, 'Receive the Holy Spirit'" (John 20:22 NKJV).

Recite God's words, "Be still, and know that I am God" (Psalm 46:10 NKJV). Before you know it, you will feel yourself connected with the Holy Spirit (which, in Hebrew, is *ruakh*, meaning "wind" or "air in motion"). Pray, "Lord, in this breath I come to You. Bring peace to my soul and spirit. Calm me, Your daughter, within and without."

Stress Less, Pray More

Trusting in God

Unto thee, O Lord, do I lift up my soul. O my God, I trust in thee. . . . Lead me in thy truth, and teach me: for thou art the God of my salvation; on thee do I wait all the day. . . . The meek will he guide in judgment: and the meek will he teach his way. . . . What man is he that feareth the Lord? him shall he teach in the way that he shall choose. His soul shall dwell at ease; and his seed shall inherit the earth.

Psalm 25:1–2, 5, 9, 12–13 KJV

Do you trust God to make decisions for you? Do you believe He has your best interests at heart? Are you meek enough to accept God to do things His way and in His timing?

When you allow God to choose your path, when you believe in His love for you, when you submit to His way, timing, and reasonings, you'll find God's guidance in every decision you make—and the peace that comes with trusting Him for everything.

Today, lift up your soul to God. Bring Him your worries, issues, plans, and quandaries. Then pray today's nine-word prayer as you go through this day and every day, leaving all in His good hands.

365 Devotions on the Power of Prayer

Dear God, you choose. I choose what you choose.

S. D. Gordon

Night Watches

My whole being shall be satisfied. . .when I remember You upon my bed and meditate on You in the night watches. For You have been my help, and in the shadow of Your wings will I rejoice. My whole being follows hard after You and clings closely to You; Your right hand upholds me.

Psalm 63:5–8 AMPC

It's late at night, and you should be fast asleep. But for some reason, you're still awake. In the quiet darkness, it's easy to let your mind wander into the even darker territory of worry. But why not switch up your thought pattern and go from worry to wonder by meditating on God. Remember how much God has done for you. How He protected and cared for you, helped you, and provided all you needed to make it to this point in your day and in your life. Rejoice in and thank Him for all the blessings He has bestowed upon you. Then see yourself clinging to Him as He holds you up, carries you, and pours out upon you His strength and peace.

Worry Less, Pray More

To desire God is to have him. To long for him is to be at the well-head. To remember him on the bed rests us. To meditate on him in the night is to have the dawn. The shadow of his wings is absolute safety.

God is always in front of us. The Savior went before; we must follow in his steps, but there ought to be as little space as possible. Another turn of the road, and you will see him!

F. B. MEYER, *Bible Commentary*

Peace Within

I have told you these things, so that in Me you may have [perfect] peace and confidence. In the world you have tribulation and trials and distress and frustration; but be of good cheer [take courage; be confident, certain, undaunted]! For I have overcome the world.

John 16:33 AMPC

Jesus knows you'll have times of trouble. Yet as you live in Him, you'll find that perfect peace and confidence you need to face them. So, no matter what has happened, is happening, or may happen, don't worry. Instead, take courage. Live the life God has planned for you. Have confidence in Jesus and have peace within because He has overcome your world. He says, "I have deprived it of power to harm you and have conquered it for you" (John 16:33 AMPC). As you go about your tasks today, give Jesus full access of heart, mind, body, spirit, and soul. Allow His peace to reign over you. In Him, you will become an overcomer.

Worry Less, Pray More

Jesus comforts the disciples with a promise of peace in Him by virtue of His victory over the world, whatever troubles they might meet within it. . . .

His departure from them was really for the best. It is the will of Christ that His disciples should have peace within, whatever their troubles may be. Peace in Christ is the only true peace. Through Him we have peace with God, and so in Him we have peace in our own minds. The Word of Christ aims at this.

MATTHEW HENRY

That Interior Peace

So let God work his will in you.

James 4:7 MSG

You may not have much control over your exterior life, but you do have control over your interior life. To find that wonderful peace within, you need both faith and prayer.

At the beginning of each day, declare to God that you desire to belong to Him entirely, and that you will devote yourself wholly to acquiring the spirit of prayer and of the interior life.

Make it your chief study to conform yourself to the will of God even in the smallest things, saying in the midst of the most annoying contradictions and with the most alarming prospects for the future: "My God, I desire with all my heart to do Your holy will; I submit in all things and absolutely to Your good pleasure for time and eternity, I wish to do this, O God, for two reasons: first, because You are my Sovereign Lord and it is but just that Your will should be accomplished; second, because I am convinced by faith and by experience that Your will is in all things as good and beneficent as it is just and adorable, while my own desire is corrupt, because I nearly always long for what would do me harm. Therefore, from this time forward, I renounce my own will to follow Your will in all things; dispose of me, O God, according to Your good will and pleasure."

This continual practice of submission will preserve that interior peace as the foundation of the spiritual life.

JEAN-PIERRE DE CAUSSADE